CAMBRIDGE LIBRARY COLLECTION

Books of enduring scholarly value

Education

This series focuses on educational theory and practice, particularly in the context of eighteenth- and nineteenth-century Europe and its colonies, and America. During this period, the questions of who should be educated, to what age, to what standard and using what curriculum, were widely debated. The reform of schools and universities, the drive towards improving women's education, and the movement for free (or at least low-cost) schools for the poor were all major concerns both for governments and for society at large. The books selected for reissue in this series discuss key issues of their time, including the 'appropriate' levels of instruction for the children of the working classes, the emergence of adult education movements, and proposals for the higher education of women. They also cover topics that still resonate today, such as the nature of education, the role of universities in the diffusion of knowledge, and the involvement of religious groups in establishing and running schools.

A Father's Instructions

A physician and medical reformer enthused by the scientific and cultural progress of the Enlightenment as it took hold in Britain, Thomas Percival (1740–1804) wrote on many topics, including public health and demography. His volume on medical ethics is considered the first modern formulation, and it and several others of his works are reissued in this series. This short book of improving tales, first published in 1777, and revised and enlarged in 1779, was originally written for his own children, and, as he says, the articles 'are placed in the order in which they were written … as leisure allowed, or as the subjects of them were suggested'. The little stories contain lessons, on obedience to parents, family affection, and kindness to animals, among many other examples of moral instruction. Percival refers to the book as 'Part the First', but a further collection seems never to have been published.

T0381807

Cambridge University Press has long been a pioneer in the reissuing of out-of-print titles from its own backlist, producing digital reprints of books that are still sought after by scholars and students but could not be reprinted economically using traditional technology. The Cambridge Library Collection extends this activity to a wider range of books which are still of importance to researchers and professionals, either for the source material they contain, or as landmarks in the history of their academic discipline.

Drawing from the world-renowned collections in the Cambridge University Library and other partner libraries, and guided by the advice of experts in each subject area, Cambridge University Press is using state-of-the-art scanning machines in its own Printing House to capture the content of each book selected for inclusion. The files are processed to give a consistently clear, crisp image, and the books finished to the high quality standard for which the Press is recognised around the world. The latest print-on-demand technology ensures that the books will remain available indefinitely, and that orders for single or multiple copies can quickly be supplied.

The Cambridge Library Collection brings back to life books of enduring scholarly value (including out-of-copyright works originally issued by other publishers) across a wide range of disciplines in the humanities and social sciences and in science and technology.

A Father's Instructions

Consisting of Moral Tales, Fables, and Reflections

THOMAS PERCIVAL

CAMBRIDGE
UNIVERSITY PRESS

University Printing House, Cambridge, CB2 8BS, United Kingdom

Cambridge University Press is part of the University of Cambridge.

It furthers the University's mission by disseminating knowledge in the pursuit of
education, learning and research at the highest international levels of excellence.

www.cambridge.org
Information on this title: www.cambridge.org/9781108077590

© in this compilation Cambridge University Press 2017

This edition first published 1779
This digitally printed version 2017

ISBN 978-1-108-07759-0 Paperback

This book reproduces the text of the original edition. The content and language reflect
the beliefs, practices and terminology of their time, and have not been updated.

Cambridge University Press wishes to make clear that the book, unless originally published
by Cambridge, is not being republished by, in association or collaboration with,
or with the endorsement or approval of, the original publisher or its successors in title.

A

FATHER's INSTRUCTIONS;

CONSISTING OF

MORAL TALES, FABLES,

AND

REFLECTIONS.

———————

PART THE FIRST.

———————

TO

THE RIGHT HONOURABLE

THE

COUNTESS of STAMFORD;

AN AMIABLE PATTERN

OF FILIAL PIETY,

CONJUGAL AFFECTION,

AND MATERNAL LOVE;

THESE

MORAL TALES

ARE INSCRIBED,

AS A

TRIBUTE OF ESTEEM AND RESPECT,

BY HER LADYSHIP'S

MOST FAITHFUL,

AND MOST OBEDIENT SERVANT,

THE AUTHOR.

T O

T. B. P. — A. P. — F. P.
J. P. &c.

MY DEAR CHILDREN,

THE little prefent which
is now offered to your
acceptance, if it have no other
value, will at leaft evince the
fincerity and warmth of my
affection for you. It will fhew
that you have been the objects
of my fondeft attention, and
tendereft folicitude. The buf-
tle

tle of the town, and the anxie-
ties of an active profeſſion have
indeed neceſſarily diverted my
thoughts, and at times ex-
cluded your image from my
mind; but, like the bird which
you have hunted from her neſt,
my heart has ſoon returned to
the place where all its pleaſing
cares are centred. In our delightful retirement at Hart-Hill,
every thing around me has con-
ſpired to ſuggeſt ideas of your
health, your happineſs, or improvement. The ſetting ſun,
the ſhady tree, the whiſpering
breeze, or the fragrant flower
have alike furniſhed ſome tale
or analogy, which has been applied to your inſtruction.

WHEN

WHEN you recollect thefe
Leffons of Wifdom and Virtue,
I flatter myfelf you will affoci-
ate with them the paternal endearments with which they were
delivered ; and that I fhall live
with honour in your memories,
when forgotten by the world,
and mouldering in the duft.
Such immortality I am more
ambitious to obtain, than all
the fame which learning or philofophy beftows.

ADIEU ! my dear children.
May you be wife, virtuous, and
happy ! And hereafter may we
meet, to part no more, in thofe
regions of the bleffed, where
our

our knowledge and felicity will be for ever increaſing ; and where we ſhall enjoy together the glorious preſence of our common Father, the Parent of the Univerſe !

THOMAS PERCIVAL.

HART-HILL, near MANCHESTER,
Auguſt 1ſt, 1775.

P R E F A C E.

AS the following Tales and Reflections will fall into other
hands befides thofe of the author's
children, for whofe ufe they were
folely intended; it may be proper
to acquaint the reader, that three
objects of inftruction have been prin-
cipally kept in view. The firft and
leading one is to refine the feelings
of the heart, and to infpire the mind
with the love of moral excellence.
And furely nothing can operate more
forcibly, than ftriking pictures of
the

the beauty of virtue, and the deformity of vice; which at once convince the judgment, and leave a laft-
ing impreffion on the imagination.
Dry precepts are little attended to,
and foon forgotten *(a)*: And if in-
culcated with feverity, they produce
in youth an averfion to every fubject
of ferious reflection; teaching them,
as Erafmus juftly obferves, *virtutem
fimul odiffe et noffe.*

THE fecond defign of this little
work is to awaken curiofity, to excite the fpirit of inquiry, and to convey in a lively and entertaining manner, a knowledge of the works of
God. On this account a ftrict attention has been paid to truth and
nature. No improbabilities are related.

(a) LONGUM iter per præcepta; breve et efficax
per exempla.

SENECA.

ted, and moſt of the narrations are
conformable to the uſual courſe of
things, or derived from the records
of hiſtory.

THE third end propoſed is to promote a more early acquaintance with
the uſe of words and idioms. Theſe
being only the arbitrary marks of our
ideas, ſuch as are moſt proper and ex-
preſſive may be learned, with no leſs
facility, than the vulgar and familiar forms of ſpeech.

IT will be acknowledged that theſe
are highly intereſting and important
objects; but the attainment of them
muſt depend upon the attention of
the learner, and the capacity of his
parent or tutor to explain the terms,
point out the analogies, and enforce
the reflections which are here delivered. To the younger pupil, therefore,

fore, every tale that is fuited to his years, fhould be made a diftinct leffon, and a reafonable time allotted for the fulleft illuftration of it. And when the words, the fubject, and the moral are clearly underftood, his curiofity concerning whatever may be connected with, or fuggefted by them, fhould be gratified and encouraged.

Such an early exertion of almoft every faculty of the mind, cannot fail to enliven the imagination, quicken the apprehenfion, enlarge the underftanding, and give ftrength and folidity to the judgment. And thefe are the moft valuable advantages which can be derived from the completeft education. For half of what we learn in youth is foon loft in oblivion; and ferves only for the exercife and improvement of our capacities.

capacities. So limited indeed are
the powers of memory, that every
man of letters may apply to himſelf,
what Dr. Bentley ſaid of Dr. Gooch,
with a pride diſgraceful to learning,
I have FORGOTTEN *more knowledge
than he* POSSESSES.

THE compoſition of Themes generally forms a part of the ſyſtem of
education in public ſchools. But
the taſk is always irkſome to boys,
and ſeldom well executed by them;
becauſe a grave, didactic, and me-
thodical diſcourſe is not ſuited to
their taſte and genius. The writing
of tales and fables, with moral reflections, might perhaps be a more
uſeful and entertaining exerciſe; as
it would afford a greater latitude for
invention, would better diſplay the
powers of imagination, and would
produce the happy talent of relating
familiar

familiar and trivial occurrences with eafe and elegance.

No attention has been paid to fyftem, in the arrangement of the articles contained in this volume. They are placed in the order in which they were written ; and they were written at various times, as leifure allowed, or as the fubjects of them were fuggefted, by family incidents, and other fortuitous circumftances. But though the tales are feverally adapted to certain ages and occafions, it is hoped that their utility will not be confined within fuch precife and narrow limits. The amufements and inftructions, even of early youth, are reviewed in manhood with fatisfaction and advantage. And as the fame objects, at different periods of life, excite different ideas and reflections, the leffons which are comprehenfible to an

intelligent

intelligent boy of ten, may furnifh new matter to him at twenty, and be interefting to others of every age. *(a)*

PERHAPS fome apology may be thought neceffary for the publication of a work, in many refpects of a private nature, and profeffedly written by a parent, for the inftruction only of his own children. The author chufes not to plead, though he might with truth, the folicitation of his moft judicious friends, who have honoured his undertaking with their approbation. He relies on the candour of the public; confcious that he is influenced by no other motive than a fincere defire to do good. And he flatters himfelf

b   that

(a) " I READ in Livy, fays Montaigne, what
" another man does not; and Plutarch read in him
" what I do not."

that precepts which have flowed
from the heart, will reach the heart,
and produce impreſſions on the tender minds of youth not to be expected from the wiſeſt maxims, delivered
with coldneſs and indifference.

*Quamobrem, pergite, Adoleſcentes,
atque in ſtudia incumbite, ut et vobis
honori, et amicis utilitati, et Reipublicæ emolumento eſſe poſſitis (b).*

(b) Cicero.

T H E

THE

CONTENTS.

PART THE FIRST.

The additional Articles in this Volume are marked with Afterifks.

THE CONTENTS.

PART

PART THE FIRST.

The

The CONTENTS. xxiii

E R R A T A.

Page 145, line 5, for *of all* read *over all*.
    227,   10, for *threſh* read *thraſh*.
    240,   12, for *each belongs* read *all belong*.
For *deſarts* in various places read *deſerts*.

MORAL

TALES, FABLES,

AND

REFLECTIONS.

HÆC SCRIPSI NON OTIJ ABUNDANTIA, SED'
AMORIS ERGA TE.

CIC. EPIST.

MORAL
TALES, FABLES,
AND
REFLECTIONS.

IDLENESS and IRRESOLUTION.

HORACE, a celebrated Roman Poet, relates that a country man, who wanted to paſs a river, ſtood loitering on the banks of it, in the fooliſh expectation that a current ſo rapid, would ſoon diſcharge its waters. But the ſtream ſtill flowed, increaſed, perhaps, by freſh torrents from the mountains; and it muſt for ever flow, becauſe the ſources from which it is derived are inexhauſtible.

THUS

Thus the *idle and irresolute youth* trifles over his books, or waftes in play his precious moments; deferring the tafk of improvement, which at firft is eafy to be accomplifhed, but which wiil become more and more difficult, the longer it be neglected.

CRUELTY to INSECTS.

MR. Melmoth, in one of his elegant letters, informs his friend, that the fnails have had more than their fhare of his peaches and nectarines this feafon; but that he deems it a fort of cruelty to fuffer them to be deftroyed. It feems to be his opinion, that it is no lefs inhuman to crufh to death a harmlefs infect, whofe only offence is that he eats the food which nature has provided for his fuftenance, than it would be to kill a more bulky creature for the fame reafon. For the fenfations of many infects are, at leaft, as exquifite as thofe of animals of more enlarged dimenfions.

The

The Millepedes rolls itfelf round upon the flighteft touch; and the Snail draws in her horns upon the firft approach of the hand. Such inftances of fenfibility certainly confirm the obfervation of our inimitable Shakefpear, who teaches us that

— the poor beetle which we tread upon,
In corporal fufferance feels a pang as great
As when a giant dies.

But whilft we encourage thefe amiable feelings of the heart, we muft not forget that humanity itfelf may be carried to an unreafonable, and even ridiculous extreme. Mr. Bayle relates that Bellarmine, a Romifh Saint, patiently fuffered the fleas, and other vermin, to prey upon him. *We fhall have Heaven,* faid he, *to reward us for our fufferings; but thefe poor creatures have only the enjoyment of the prefent life.*

AFFECTION to PARENTS.

AN amiable youth was lamenting, in terms of the fincereft grief, the death

of

of a moſt affectionate parent. His companion endeavoured to conſole him by the reflection, that he had always behaved to the deceaſed with duty, tenderneſs, and reſpect. So I thought, replied the youth, whilſt my parent was living; but now I recollect with pain and ſorrow, many inſtances of diſobedience and neglect, for which, alas! it is too late to make atonement.

TAKING of BIRD-NESTS.

I HAVE found out a gift for my fair ;
   I have found where the wood pigeons breed.
But let me that plunder forbear !
   She will ſay 'tis a barbarous deed.

For he ne'er can be true, ſhe averr'd,
   Who can rob a poor bird of its young :
And I lov'd her the more when I heard
   Such tenderneſs fall from her tongue.

I have heard her with ſweetneſs unfold,
   How that pity was due to a dove ;
That it ever attended the bold ;
   And ſhe call'd it the ſiſter of love.

               SHENSTONE.

ON

ON THE SAME.

A BOY, who was a great deftroyer of
nefts, had carefully preferved one,
that he might enjoy the cruel pleafure of
confining in a cage the poor birds, who
had the fame natural right to liberty with
himfelf.   A hungry cat difcovered the
neft, and devoured the unfeathered brood.
The boy bewailed his lofs, and vowed revenge upon the cat; not reflecting on
the many nefts which he had *wantonly
plundered*, whilft the cat was impelled by
the dictates of nature to fatisfy a *craving
appetite*.

TENDERNESS to MOTHERS.

M ARK that parent hen; faid a father
to his beloved fon.   With what
anxious care does fhe call together her off-
fpring, and cover them with her expanded
wings!   The kite is hovering in the air,

and

and difappointed of his prey, may perhaps dart upon the hen herfelf, and bear her off in his talons!

Does not this fight fuggeft to you the tendernefs and affection of your mother? Her watchful care protected you in the helplefs period of infancy, when fhe nourifhed you with her milk, taught your limbs to move, and your tongue to lifp its unformed accents. In childhood fhe has mourned over your little griefs; has rejoiced in your innocent delights; has adminiftered to you the healing balm in ficknefs; and has inftilled into your mind the love of truth, of virtue, and of wifdom. Oh! cherifh every fentiment of refpect for fuch a mother. She merits your warmeft gratitude, efteem, and veneration.

The FOLLY of CRYING upon trifling occasions.

A LITTLE girl, who ufed to weep bitterly for the moft trifling hurt,

was

was one day attacked by a furious dog. Her cries reached the fervants of the family; but they paid little attention to what they were fo much accuftomed to hear. It happened, however, very fortunately that a country man paffed by, who, with great humanity, refcued the child from the devouring teeth of the dog.

INTEMPERANCE.

CYRUS, when a youth, being at the court of his grandfather Aftyages, undertook one day to be the cup-bearer at table. It was the duty of this officer to tafte the liquor, before it was prefented to the king. Cyrus, without performing this ceremony, delivered the cup in a very graceful manner to his grandfather. The king reminded him of his omiffion, which he imputed to forgetfulnefs. No, replied Cyrus, I was afraid to tafte, becaufe I apprehended there was poifon in the liquor: For not long fince, at an entertainment which you gave, I obferved that the lords
of

of your court, after drinking of it, became noiſy, quarrelſome, and frantic. Even you, Sir, ſeemed to have forgotten that you were a king.

XENOPHON.

CRUELTY PUNISHED.

A PACK of ravenous fox hounds were half ſtarved in their kennel, to render them more furious and eager in the chace; and were ſeverely laſhed every day by a mercileſs keeper, that they might be diſciplined to the ſtricteſt obſervance of his looks and commands. It happened that this petty tyrant entered the kennel without his ſcourge. The dogs obſerved his defenceleſs ſtate; and inſtantly flying upon him, at once ſatiated their hunger and revenge, by tearing him to pieces.

WHILST you pity the unhappy fate of the keeper, lament that, in a civilized country,

country, fuch cruelties fhould be exercifed, as to give occafion to it.

LIBERALITY.

YOU have feen the hufbandman *fcatter-ing* his feed upon the furrowed ground!
It fprings up, is gathered into his barns,
and crowns his labours with joy and plenty.—Thus the man, who *diftributes* his fortune with generofity and prudence, is am-
ply repaid by the gratitude of thofe whom
he obliges, by the approbation of his own
mind, and the favour of God.

THE PERT AND THE IGNORANT ARE PRONE TO RIDICULE.

A GENTLEMAN, of a grave de-
portment, was bufily engaged in
blowing bubbles of foap and water, and
was attentively obferving them as they expanded and burft in the funfhine. A pert
youth fell into a fit of loud laughter at a
fight

fight fo ftrange, and which fhewed, as he
thought, fuch folly and infanity.—Be a-
fhamed, young man, faid one who paffed
by, of your rudenefs and ignorance.   You
now behold the greateft Philofopher of the
age, Sir Ifaac Newton, inveftigating the
nature of light and colours, by a feries of
experiments, no lefs curious than ufeful,
though you deem them childifh and infignificant.

COMPASSION to the POOR.

PITY the forrows of a poor old man,
  Whofe trembling limbs have borne him to your door,
Whofe days are dwindled to the fhorteft fpan,
  Oh! give relief, and Heaven will blefs your ftore.

Thefe tatter'd cloaths my poverty befpeak,
  Thefe hoary locks proclaim my lengthen'd years;
And many a furrow in my grief-worn cheek
  Has been the channel to a flood of tears.

Yon houfe, erected on the rifing ground,
  With tempting afpect drew me from my road;
For Plenty there a refidence has found,
  And Grandeur a magnificent abode.

Hard

Hard is the fate of the infirm and poor!
  Here, as I crav'd a morfel of their bread,
A pamper'd menial drove me from the door,
  To feek a fhelter in an humbler fhed.

Oh! take me to your hofpitable dome;
  Keen blows the wind, and piercing is the cold!
Short is my paffage to the friendly tomb,
  For I am poor and miferably old.

Should I reveal the fources of my grief,
  If foft humanity e'er touch'd your breaft,
Your hands would not withhold the kind relief,
  And tears of Pity would not be repreft.

Heaven fends misfortunes; why fhould we repine?
  'Tis Heaven has brought me to the ftate you fee;
And your condition may be foon like mine,
  The child of Sorrow, and of Mifery.

A little farm was my paternal lot,
  Then like the lark I fprightly hail'd the morn;
But ah! oppreffion forc'd me from my cot,
  My cattle dy'd, and blighted was my corn.

My daughter, once the comfort of my age,
  Lur'd by a villain from her native home,
Is caft abandon'd on the world's wide ftage,
  And doom'd in fcanty Poverty to roam.

My

My tender wife, ſweet ſoother of my care !
　Struck with ſad anguiſh at the ſtern decree,
Fell, ling'ring fell, a victim to deſpair,
　And left the world to wretchedneſs and me.

Pity the ſorrows of a poor old man,
　Whoſe trembling limbs have borne him to your door,
Whoſe days are dwindled to the ſhorteſt ſpan,
　Oh ! give relief, and Heaven will bleſs your ſtore.

THE SPEAKER, BY DR. ENFIELD.

PARENTAL AFFECTION.

THE white bear of Greenland and Spitz-
bergen is conſiderably larger than
the brown bear of Europe, or the black
bear of North America. This animal lives
upon fiſh, and ſeals, and is not only ſeen
upon land in the countries bordering on
the North Pole, but often on floats of ice,
ſeveral leagues at ſea. The following relation is copied from the *Journal of a Voyage, for making Diſcoveries towards the
North Pole.*

EARLY in the morning, the man at
the maſt head of the Carcaſe, gave notice,
that

that three bears were making their way very faft over the ice, and that they were directing their courfe towards the fhip. They had, without queftion, been invited by the fcent of the blubber of a fea horfe, killed a few days before, which the men had fet on fire, and which was burning on the ice at the time of their approach. They proved to be a fhe bear and her two cubs; but the cubs were nearly as large as the dam. They ran eagerly to the fire, and drew out from the flames part of the flefh of the fea horfe, that remained unconfumed, and ate it voracioufly. The crew from the fhip threw great lumps of the flefh of the fea horfe, which they had ftill left, upon the ice, which the old bear fetched away fingly, laid every lump before her cubs as fhe brought it, and dividing it, gave each a fhare, referving but a fmall portion to herfelf. As fhe was fetching away the laft piece, they levelled their mufkets at the cubs, and fhot them both dead; and in her retreat they wounded the dam, but not mortally.

It

It would have drawn tears of pity from any but unfeeling minds, to have marked the affectionate concern expreſſed by this poor beaſt, in the laſt moments of her expiring young. Though ſhe was ſorely wounded, and could but juſt crawl to the place where they lay, ſhe carried the lump of fleſh ſhe had fetched away, as ſhe had done others before, tore it in pieces, and laid it down before them; and when ſhe ſaw that they refuſed to eat, ſhe laid her paws firſt upon one, and then upon the other, and endeavoured to raiſe them up : all this while it was pitiful to hear her moan. When ſhe found ſhe could not ſtir them, ſhe went off, and when ſhe had gotten at ſome diſtance, looked back and moaned; and that not availing her to entice them away, ſhe returned, and ſmelling round them, began to lick their wounds. She went off a ſecond time, as before, and having crawled a few paces, looked again behind her, and for ſome time ſtood moaning. But ſtill her cubs not riſing to follow her, ſhe returned to
them

them again, and with figns of inexpreffible
fondnefs, went round one, and round the
other, pawing them, and moaning. Finding at laft that they were cold and lifelefs,
fhe raifed her head towards the fhip,
and growled a curfe upon the murderers;
which they returned with a volley of muf-
ket balls. She fell between her cubs, and
died, licking their wounds.

Can you admire the maternal affeétion
of the bear, and not feel in your heart the
warmeft emotions of gratitude, for the
ftronger and more permanent tendernefs,
you have fo long experienced from your
parents?

The FALLACY of EXTERNAL APPEAR-
ANCE.

IS there any hidden beauty, faid Alexis
to Euphronius, in that dufky, ill fhap-
ed ftone, which you examine with fo much
attention? I am admiring the wonderful

C

properties,

properties, not the beauty, replied Euphronius, which it poffeffes. It is by
means of this ftone that the mariner fteers
his tracklefs courfe through the vaft ocean;
and without it the fpices of the Eaft, the
mines of Peru, and all the luxuries which
commerce pours into Europe, would for
ever have remained unknown. — The curiofity of Alexis was excited, and he was
impatient to learn in what wonderful manner fuch advantages could be derived from
a fubftance, apparently of fo little value.
— This magnet or loadftone, for it is
known by both names, faid Euphronius,
imparts to iron the property of fettling itfelf, when nicely balanced, in a direction
nearly North and South. The failor is
therefore furnifhed with an unerring guide
in the midft of the ocean. For when he
faces the North, the Eaft and Weft are
readily afcertained, the former lying to his
right, and the latter to his left hand.
And from thefe four points, all the fubdivifions of the mariner's compafs are
formed. The figure of a ftar, which
you

you fo often draw upon paper, will give you a clear idea of the compafs. Make yourfelf a mafter of it; and from the prefent inftance of your want of knowledge, learn a becoming modefty in the judgments which you form concerning the productions of nature. The whole creation is the workmanfhip of an Omnipotent Being; and though we cannot always trace the marks of harmony, beauty, or ufefulnefs, yet doubtlefs to the eye of a fuperior intelligence, every part of it difplays infallible wifdom, and unbounded goodnefs.

SELFISH SORROW REPROVED.

IT was a holiday in the month of June, and Alexis had prepared himfelf to fet out, with a party of his companions, upon a little journey of pleafure. But the fky lowered, the clouds gathered, and he remained for fome time in anxious fufpenfe about his expedition; which at laft was prevented by heavy and continu-

ed

ed rain.   The difappointment overpowered his fortitude ; he burft into tears ; lamented the untimely change of weather ;
and fullenly refufed all confolation.

In the evening the clouds were dif-
perfed ; the fun fhone with unufual brightnefs ; and the face of nature feemed to be renewed in vernal beauty. Euphronius conducted Alexis into the fields.   The ftorm
of paffion in his breaft was now ftilled ;
and the ferenity of the air, the mufic of
the feathered fongfters, the verdure of the
meadows, and the fweet perfumes which
breathed around, regaled every fenfe, and
filled his mind with peace and joy.

Don't you remark, faid Euphronius,
the delightful change which has fuddenly
taken place in the whole creation ? Recollect the appearance of the fcene before
us yefterday.   The ground was then
parched with a long drought ; the flowers hid their drooping heads ; no fragrant odours were perceived ;   and ve-
getation

getation feemed to ceafe. To what caufe muft we impute the revival of nature? — To the rain which fell this morning, replied Alexis with a modeft confufion. He was ftruck with the felfifhnefs and folly of his conduct; and his own bitter reflections anticipated the reproofs of Euphronius.

HONESTY and GENEROSITY.

A POOR man, who was door-keeper to a houfe in Milan, found a purfe which contained two hundred crowns. The man who had loft it, informed by a public advertifement, came to the houfe, and giving fufficient proof that the purfe belonged to him, the door-keeper reftored it. Full of joy and gratitude, the owner offered his benefactor twenty crowns, which he abfolutely refufed. Ten were then propofed, and afterwards five; but the door-keeper ftill continuing inexorable, the man threw his purfe upon

the

the ground, and in an angry tone cried,
" I have loft nothing, nothing at all, if
you thus refufe to accept of a gratuity."
The door-keeper then confented to receive
five crowns, which he immediately diftributed amongft the poor.

ROLLIN.

A GENEROUS RETURN FOR AN INJURY.

WHEN the great Condè commanded
the Spanifh army, and laid fiege
to one of the French towns in Flanders, a
foldier being ill treated by a general officer,
and ftruck feveral times with a cane, for
fome difrefpeftful words he had let fall,
anfwered very coolly, that he fhould foon
make him repent of it. Fifteen days afterwards, the fame general officer ordered the
colonel of the trenches to find a bold and
intrepid fellow, to execute an important
enterprife, for which he promifed a reward of a hundred piftoles. The foldier
we are fpeaking of, who paffed for the

braveft

braveſt in the regiment, offerẹd his ſervice, and going with thirty of his comrades, which he had the liberty to make choice of, he diſcharged a very hazardous com-miſſion, with incredible courage and good fortune. Upon his return the general officer highly commended him, and gave him the hundred piſtoles which he had promiſed. The ſoldier preſently diſtri-buted them amongſt his comrades, ſaying he did not ſerve for pay, and demanded only that if his late action ſeemed to deſerve any recompenſe, they would make him an officer. And now ſir, adds he to the general, who did not know him, I am the ſoldier whom you abuſed ſo much fifteen days ago, and I then told you I would make you repent of it. The general in great admiration, and melt-ing into tears, threw his arms around his neck, begged his pardon, and gave him a commiſſion that very day.

ROLLIN.

WE TOO OFTEN JUDGE OF MEN BY THE
SPLENDOUR, AND NOT BY THE ME-
RIT OF THEIR ACTIONS.

ALEXANDER demanded of a Pirate,
whom he had taken, by what right
he infested the seas? By the same right,
replied he boldly, that you enslave the
world. But I am called a robber, because
I have only one small vessel; and you are
styled a conqueror, because you command
great fleets and armies.

CICERO.

SILENCE AND RESERVE REPROVED.

SOPHRON *(a)* was frequently the
companion of Euphronius in his
various journeys. He was a youth of
observation, but indulged too much a
natural reserve of temper. His cousins
com-

(a) The Author's Nephew.

complained that he who so often enjoyed amusement himself, should contribute so little to the general entertainment of the family. At first they intended to petition Euphronius to carry him no more abroad ; but a good-natured stratagem answered better the purpose of reproof. They agreed that each should pursue, for a few days, a conduct similar to that of Sophron. One visited the magnificent Museum of Mr. Lever at Alkrington; another went to a very diverting Comedy; and a third sailed, with a party, upon the Duke of Bridgewater's Canal, and viewed all the wonders of that stupendous undertaking. But when they returned home, the chearful communications of friendship were suppressed; and the usual eagerness to disclose all which they had seen, was converted into silence and reserve. No social converse enlivened the evening hours, and the sprightliness of youth gave place to mute solemnity. Sophron remarked the change with surprise and solicitude. He felt the loss of that

gaiety

gaiety and unreferved intercourfe, which he feldom promoted, but of which he loved to participate. And when the defign of his coufins was explained to him, he candidly acknowledged, and promifed to amend his fault.

CRUELTY TO INSECTS.

A CERTAIN youth indulged himfelf in the cruel entertainment of torturing and killing flies. He tore off their wings and legs, and then watched with pleafure their impotent efforts to efcape from him. Sometimes he collected a number of them together, and crufhed them at once to death; glorying, like many a celebrated hero, in the devaftation he committed. Alexis remonftrated with him, in vain, on this barbarous conduct. He could not perfuade him to believe that flies are capable of pain, and have a right, no
lefs

lefs than ourfelves, to life, liberty, and enjoyment. The figns of agony, which, when tormented, they exprefs by the quick and various contortions of their bodies, he neither underftood nor would attend to.

Alexis had a mifcrofcope; and he defired his companion, one day, to examine a moft beautiful and furprifing animal. Mark, faid he, how it is ftudded from head to tail with black and filver, and its body all over befet with the moft curious briftles! The head contains a pair of lively eyes, encircled with filver hairs; and the trunk confifts of two parts, which fold over each other. The whole body is ornamented with plumes and decorations, which furpafs all the luxuries of drefs, in the courts of the greateft princes. Pleafed and aftonifhed with what he faw, the youth was impatient to know the name and properties of this wonderful animal. It was withdrawn from the magnifier; and when offered to his naked eye,

proved

proved to be a poor fly, which had been the victim of his wanton cruelty.

THE HONOUR AND ADVANTAGE OF A CON-
STANT ADHERENCE TO TRUTH.

PETRARCH, a celebrated Italian Poet who flourished about four hundred years ago, recommended himself to the confidence and affection of Cardinal Colonna, in whose family he resided, by his candour and strict regard to truth. A violent quarrel occurred in the houshold of this nobleman, which was carried so far that they had recourse to arms. The Cardinal wished to know the foundation of this affair; and that he might be able to decide with justice, he assembled all his people, and obliged them to bind themselves by a most solemn oath on the Gospels, to declare the whole truth. Every one, without exception, submitted to this determination; even the Bishop of Luna, brother to the Cardinal, was not excused.

excufed. Petrarch, in his turn, prefenting himfelf to take the oath, the Cardinal clofed the book, and faid, " *As to you, Petrarch, your word is fufficient.*" *(a)*

A STORY fimilar to this is related of Zenocrates, an Athenian Philofopher, who lived three hundred years before Chrift, and was educated in the fchool of Plato. The people of Athens entertained fo high an opinion of his probity, that one day when he approached the altar, to confirm by an oath the truth of what he had afferted, the judges unanimoufly declared his word to be fufficient evidence.

SLOTH CONTRASTED WITH INDUSTRY.

THE Sloth is an animal of South America, and is fo ill formed for motion, that a few paces are often the journey of a week; and fo indifpofed to move,

---

(a) See the Life of Petrarch, elegantly tranflated by Mrs. Dobfon.

move, that he never changes his place, but when impelled by the fevereſt ſtings of hunger. He lives upon the leaves, fruit, and flowers of trees, and often on the bark itſelf, when nothing beſides is left for his ſubſiſtence. As a large quantity of food is neceſſary for his ſupport, he generally ſtrips a tree of all its verdure in leſs than a fortnight. And being then deſtitute of food, he drops down, like a lifeleſs maſs, from the branches to the ground. After remaining torpid ſome time, from the ſhock received by the fall, he prepares for a journey to ſome neighbouring tree, to which he crawls with a motion almoſt imperceptible. At length arrived, he aſcends the trunk, and devours, with famiſhed appetite, whatever the branches afford. By conſuming the bark he ſoon deſtroys the life of the tree, and thus the ſource is loſt from which his ſuſtenance is derived.

SUCH is the miſerable ſtate of this ſlothful animal. How different are the
comforts

comforts and enjoyments of the induftrious Beaver! This creature is found
in the northern parts of America, and
is about two feet long and one foot high.
The figure of it fomewhat refembles that
of a rat. In the months of June and July
the beavers affemble, and form a fociety
which generally confifts of more than two
hundred. They always fix their abode by
the fide of a lake or river; and in order to
make a dead water in that part which lies
above and below, they erect with incredible
labour, a dam or pier, perhaps fourfcore
or a hundred feet long, and ten or twelve
feet thick at the bafe. When this dike is
compleated, they build their feveral apart-
ments, which are divided into three ftories.
The firft is below the level of the mole,
and is for the moft part full of water.
The walls of their habitations are perpen-
dicular, and about two feet thick : If any
wood project from them, they cut it off
with their teeth, which are more ferrice-
able than faws. And by the help of their
tails, they plaifter all their works with a
kind

kind of mortar, which they prepare of dry grafs and clay mixed together. In Auguft or September they begin to lay up their ftores of food ; which confift of the wood of the birch, the plane, and of fome other trees. Thus they pafs the gloomy winter in eafe and plenty.

Thefe two American animals, contrafted with each other, afford a moft ftriking picture of the bleffings of induftry, and the penury and wretchednefs of floth.

The FOLLY and ODIOUSNESS of AFFECTATION.

LUCY, Emilia, and Sophronia, feated on a bank of daifies, near a purling ftream, were liftening to the mufic of a neighbouring grove. The fun gilded with his fetting beams the weftern fky, gentle zephyrs breathed around, and the feathered fongfters feemed to vie with each other in their evening notes of gratitude and praife.

Delighted

Delighted with the artlefs melody of the linnet, the goldfinch, the woodlark, and the thruſh, they were all *ear*, and obſerved not a peacock, which had ſtrayed from a diftant farm, and was approaching them with a majeftic pace and expanded plumage. The harmony of the concert was foon interrupted by the loud and harſh cries of this ſtately bird; which though chafed away by Emilia, continued his vociferations with the confidence that confcious beauty too often infpires. Does this foolifh bird, faid Lucy, fancy that he is qualified to fing, becaufe he is furnifhed with a fpreading tail, ornamented with the richeft colours? I know not, replied Sophronia, whether the peacock be capable of fuch a reflection; but I hope that you and Emilia will always avoid the difplay of whatever is inconfiftent with your fex, your ftation, or your character. Shun affectation in all its odious forms; affume no borrowed airs; and be content to pleafe, to ſhine, or to be ufeful, in the way which nature points out, and which reafon approves.

D   The

The Passions should be governed by Reason.

SOPHRON and Alexis had frequently heard Euphronius mention the experiment of ftilling the waves with oil, made by his friend Doctor Franklin. They were impatient to repeat it; and a brisk wind proving favourable to the trial, they hastened, one evening, to a sheet of water in the pleasure grounds of Eugenio, near Hart-Hill. The oil was scattered upon the pool, and spread itself instantly on all sides, calming the whole surface of the water, and reflecting the most beautiful colours. Elated with success the youths returned to Euphronius, to enquire the cause of such a wonderful appearance. He informed them that the wind blowing upon water which is covered with a coat of oil, slides over the surface of it, and produces no friction that can raise a wave. But this curious philosophical fact, said he, suggests a most im-

                                                            portant

portant moral reflection. When you fuffer yourfelves to be ruffled by paffion, your
minds refemble the *puddle in a ftorm*. But
reafon if you hearken to her voice, will
then, like oil poured upon the water, calm
the turbulence within you, and reftore you
to ferenity and peace.

AFFECTION EXTENDED TO INANIMATE OBJECTS.

A Beautiful tree grew, in an open
fpace, oppofite to the parlour windows of Euphronius's houfe. It was an
object which his family often contemplated with pleafure. The verdant foli-
age, with which it was covered, gave
an early indication of fpring; its fpreading
branches furnifhed an agreeable fhade,
and tempered the heat of the noon-tide
fun; and the falling leaves, in autumn,
marked the varying feafons, and warned
them of the approach of winter. One
D 2   lucklefs

lucklefs morning the ax was laid to the root of this admired tree; and it fell a lamented victim to the rage for building, which depopulates the country, and multiplies mifery, difeafes, and death, by the enlargement of great towns.

You now feel, faid Euphronius to Alexis on this occafion, the force of that good-natured remark of Mr. Addifon, in one of the Spectators, that he fhould not care to have an old ftump pulled up, which he had remembered ever fince he was a child. The affections of a generous heart are extended, by the early affociation of ideas, to almoft every furrounding object. Hence the delight which we receive from revifiting thofe fcenes, in which we paffed our youth; the fchool where our firft friendfhips were formed; or the academic groves in which fair fcience unveiled herfelf to our enraptured view.

SUETO-

Suetonius relates, that the Roman Emperor Vespasian went constantly every year, to pass the summer in a small country house near Rieti, where he was born, and to which he would never add any embellishment: And that Titus, his successor, was carried thither in his last illness, to die in the place where his father had begun and ended his days. The Emperor Pertinax, says Capitolinus, during the time of his abode in Liguria, lodged in his father's house; and raising a great number of magnificent buildings around it, he left the cottage in the midst, a striking monument of his delicacy of sentiment, and greatness of soul.

A TRIBUTE to FRIENDSHIP; and a PATTERN for IMITATION.

YOU were lamenting the other day, my dear Alexis, the loss of a beautiful tree, cut down in its prime, and when

D 3   crowned

crowned with all its leafy honours. I am
now mourning, continued Euphronius, a
more diftrefsful and untimely ftroke, which
has fevered from me Philander, the coun-
fellor of my youth, and the friend and
companion of my riper years. He poffeffed a folid judgment and enlarged underftanding, and, what is rarely found
united with them, a lively imagination,
a quick conception, and refined tafte.
His knowledge was rather general and
extenfive than profound; but his ideas
were fo well arranged, that he had them
always at command, and could converfe
on every fubject with eafe, propriety, and
even mafterly fkill. His pulpit compofitions were rational, nervous, and pathetic;
his delivery was manly, animated, and affecting. Strongly impreffed himfelf with
the divine truths of religion, and the facred
obligations of morality, he enforced them
on the minds of his audience with an energy, irrefiftibly perfuafive. An affemblage
of virtues conftituted his moral character.

His

His heart was tenderneſs and humanity itſelf; his friendſhip warm, ſteady, and diſintereſted; his benevolence univerſal; and his integrity inviolate. Nor were theſe the untried virtues of retirement; for he was early engaged in the active ſcenes of life, and aſſaulted with difficulties which required the utmoſt fortitude to ſurmount. — He was not deficient in thoſe exterior accompliſhments, which add charms to virtue, and make goodneſs ſhine with ſuperior luſtre. His manners were poliſhed, his addreſs was eaſy and engaging, and his converſation ſprightly, entertaining, and inſtructive. As a gentleman, a ſcholar, a preacher, a companion, and a friend, he was almoſt without an equal.

Though my heart bleeds at the recollection of the loſs which I have ſuſtained, yet I feel a pleaſure, my Alexis, in bringing to your knowledge the virtues of ſuch a character. Venerate the

D 4 memory,

memory, and copy the bright example
of Philander. *(b)*

(b) THE following infcription was defigned for the monument of Philander.

NEAR THIS PLACE

LIE

THE REMAINS

OF

THE REVEREND ————

————————

MINISTER OF THIS CONGREGATION ;

TO

WHICH HE WAS ENDEARED

BY

A FAITHFUL AND AFFECTIONATE

DISCHARGE

OF

THE PASTORAL OFFICE;

BY

HIS CHEARFUL PIETY,

UNIVERSAL BENEVOLENCE,

EXTENSIVE KNOWLEDGE,

AND

TEMPERATE ZEAL

FOR

CIVIL AND RELIGIOUS LIBERTY.

HE DIED JANUARY 22, 1770. AGED 45.

" HEU ! QUANTO MINUS EST,
" CUM RELIQUIS VERSARI,
" QUAM TUI
" MEMINISSE."

SCEP-

SCEPTICISM CONDEMNED.

SOPHRON afferted that he could hear the flighteft fcratch of a pin, at the diftance of ten yards. It is *impoffible*, faid Alexis, and immediately appealed to Euphronius, who was walking with them. Though I do not believe, replied Euphronius, that Sophron's ears are more acute than yours, yet I difapprove of your hafty decifion concerning the *impoffibility* of what you fo little underftand. You are ignorant of the nature of found, and of the various means by which it may be increafed, or quickened in its progrefs; and modefty fhould lead you, in fuch a cafe, to fufpend your judgment till you have made the proper and neceffary inquiries. An opportunity now prefents itfelf, which will afford Sophron the fatisfaction he defires. Place your ear at one end of this long rafter of dale timber, and I will fcratch the other end with a pin. Alexis obeyed,

and

and diftinctly heard the found; which being conveyed through the tubes of the wood, was augmented in loudnefs, as in a fpeaking trumpet, or the horn of the huntfman.

Scepticism and credulity are equally unfavourable to the acquifition of knowledge. The latter anticipates, and the former precludes all enquiry. One leaves the mind fatisfied with error, the other with ignorance.

SELF-GOVERNMENT.

EURIPIADES, the Lacedemonian, Generaliffimo of the Greek forces employed againft the Perfians, was enraged that Themiftocles, a young man, and the chief of the Athenians, fhould prefume to oppofe his opinion, and lifted up his cane to ftrike him. Themiftocles, without emotion, cried out, *ftrike, and welcome, if you will but hear me!* Euripiades, furprifed

at

at his calmnefs and prefence of mind, liftened to his advice, and obtained that
famous victory in the Straights of Salamis,
which faved Greece, and conferred immortal glory on Themiftocles.

PERSONAL DEFORMITIES are not
OBJECTS of RIDICULE.

THE Dutchefs of Burgundy, when fhe
was very young, feeing an officer at
fupper who was extremely ugly, was very
loud in her ridicule of his perfon. "Ma-
dam, faid the King (Louis XIV.) to her,
I think him one of the handfomeft men
in my kingdom; for he is one of the
braveft."

VOLTAIRE.

IT is the office of REASON and PHILO-
SOPHY to MODERATE, not to SUP-
PRESS the PASSIONS.

(c) WHEN the plague raged in At-
tica, it was particularly fatal
to

(c) See Rollin's Hiftory.

to the family of Pericles, the celebrated
Athenian General. But he did not fuffer
himfelf to fink under the loffes he fuftained, and even fuppreffed every emotion
of forrow. Nature, however, at laft prevailed : For when Parabus, his only remaining child, fell a victim to this dreadful diftemper, he could no longer ftifle his
grief, which forced a flood of tears from
his eyes, whilft he was placing the crown
of flowers, as a funeral rite, upon the head
of his deceafed fon. Surely Pericles was
mifled by falfe principles of reafon and
honour, when he fuppofed that the tendernefs of the father, would fully the
glory of the conqueror ! How much more
juft was the fentiment which the Emperor
Antoninus uttered, when Marcus Aurelius
was lamenting the death of the perfon who
had educated him ? *Suffer him to indulge the
feelings of a man; for neither philofophy nor
fovereignty render us infenfible! Permitte illi
ut homo fit : neque enim vel philofophia, vel
imperium tollit affectus! (d)*

THE

(d) Julius Capitolinus.

The LOVE of FAME.

FAME is a powerful incitement to attain, and an honourable reward of fuperior excellence. But the paffion for it fhould be directed by judgment, and moderated by reafon; or we fhall be led into falfe purfuits, and betrayed into the moft difgraceful weakneffes. The wild hero, the filly fop, the affected pedant, and the extravagant virtuofo furnifh examples of the mifapplication of the love of praife. Such characters are contemplated with filent difapprobation by the Philofopher; but he laments the frailty of human nature, when he fees men of exalted virtue and abilities anxioufly courting applaufe, and proudly exulting in the acquifition of it. Who can read the Poet's exclamation on his own productions, *Exegi monumentum ære perennius:* (e) *I have raifed a monument to my glory*

(e) Hor. Od. 3.

glory more lasting than brass, without a mixture of pity and disgust? *(f)* And do we not feel similar emotions from the instances of vanity and self-commendation which abound in the writings of the first orator and greatest statesman Rome ever produced? So inordinate indeed was Cicero's love of fame, that he solicited Lucceius to write the history of his consulship, and to publish it during his life-time, *that he might be better known, and personally enjoy his honour and reputation.* He importunes him not to adhere scrupulously to the laws of history, but to make a sacrifice of truth to friendship, by speaking more to his advantage,

---

(f) THE following epitaph was composed, for himself, by Nævius a Poet, whom Cicero, in his Treatise *de Senectute,* quotes with respect; and who died in exile at Utica, in Africa, in the year of Rome 551.

> *Mortalis immortalis flere si foret fas,*
> *Flerent divæ camænæ Nævium Poetam,*
> *Itaque postquam est Orcino traditus Thesauro,*
> *Oblitei sunt Romæ loquier Latina lingua.*

> If Gods the fate of mortals might deplore,
> Each muse would weep that Nævius is no more:
> All grace of diction with the Bard is flown,
> And Rome's sweet language is in Rome unknown.

MELMOTH.

advantage, than perhaps he thought was due. *(g)* A paffion for fame like this, inftead of fupporting virtue, muft prove fubverfive of it, by ftifling thofe higher principles of morality which fhould ever influence the heart, and govern the con-duct.

GRATITUDE and PIETY.

ARTABANES was diftinguifhed with peculiar favour by a wife, powerful, and good prince. A magnificent palace, furrounded with a delightful garden, was provided for his refidence. He partook of all the luxuries of his fovereign's table, was invefted with extenfive authority, and admitted to the honour of a free intercourfe with his gracious mafter. But Artabanes was infenfible of the advantages which he enjoyed; his heart glowed not with grati-tude and refpect; he avoided the fociety of his benefactor, and abufed his bounty. —I deteft fuch a character, faid Alexis,

with

(g) Ciceronis Epift, 12, lib, 5,

with generous indignation! It is your own picture which I have drawn, replied Euphronius. The great Potentate of heaven and earth has placed you in a world, which difplays the higheft beauty, order, and magnificence; and which abounds with every means of convenience, enjoyment, and happinefs. He has furnifhed you with fuch powers of body and mind, as give you dominion over the fifhes of the fea, the fowls of the air, and the beafts of the field. And he has invited you to hold communion with him, and to exalt your own nature, by the love and imitation of his divine perfections. Yet have your eyes wandered with brutal gaze over the fair creation, unconfcious of the mighty hand from which it fprung. You have rioted in the profufion of nature, without one fecret emotion of gratitude to the fovereign difpenfer of all good. And you have flighted the glorious converfe, and forgotten the prefence of that Omnipotent Being, who fills all fpace, and exifts through all eternity.

ENVY

ENVY AND DISCONTENT.

EVER charming, ever new,
　　When will the landfcape tire the view!
The fountain's fall, the river's flow,
The woody vallies warm and low;
The windy fummit wild and high
Roughly rufhing on the fky;
The pleafant feat, the ruin'd tower,
The naked rock, the fhady bower;
The town and village, dome and farm,
Each gives each a double charm. *(b)*

ALEXIS was repeating thefe lines to Euphronius, who was reclined upon a feat in
one of his fields at Hart-Hill, enjoying
the real beauties of nature which the Poet
defcribes. The evening was ferene, and
the landfcape appeared in all the gay attire
of light and fhade. A man of lively imagination, faid Euphronius, has a property
in every thing which he fees; and you
may now conceive yourfelf to be lord of

E　　　　　the

(b) Grongar Hill, by Mr. Dyer.

the vaſt expanſe around us, and exult in
the happineſs of myriads of living creatures, who inhabit the woods, the lawns,
and mountains which preſent themſelves to
our view. The houſe, garden, and pleaſure grounds of Eugenio formed a part of
the proſpect: And Alexis expreſſed a jocular wiſh, that he had more than an imaginary property in thoſe poſſeſſions. — Ba-
niſh the ungenerous deſire, ſaid Euphronius ; for if you indulge ſuch emotions as
theſe, your heart will ſoon become a prey
to envy and diſcontent. Enjoy with gratitude the bleſſings which you have received
from the liberal hand of Providence; increaſe them, if you can with honour and
credit, by a diligent attention to the duties
of that reſpectable profeſſion, for which
you are deſigned; and though your own
cup may not be filled, rejoice that your
neighbour's overflows with plenty. Honour the abilities, and emulate the virtues
of Eugenio; but repine not that he is
wiſer, richer, or more powerful than
yourſelf. His *fortune* is expended in
acts

acts of humanity, generofity, and hofpitality: His fuperior *talents* are applied to the inftruction of his children, to the affiftance of his friends, to the encouragement of agriculture and of every ufeful art, and to fupport the caufe of liberty and the rights of mankind: And his *power* is exerted to punifh the guilty, to protect the innocent, to reward the good, and to diftribute juftice with an equal hand to all. I feel the affection of a brother for Eugenio; and efteem myfelf fingularly happy in his friendfhip.

COURAGE.

BRASIDAS, a Spartan General who was diftinguifhed for his bravery and generofity, once feized a moufe, and being bitten by it, fuffered it to efcape. *There is no animal*, faid he, *fo contemptible, but may be fafe, if it have courage to defend itfelf.*

PLUTARCH.

FALSE

FALSE AMBITION.

IT is a falſe ambition which leads men to aim at excellencies, however valuable in themſelves, that are inconſiſtent with their ſtation, character, or profeſſion; or which in the acquiſition muſt interfere with other purſuits of more importance. Nero neglected all the duties of a prince, and waſted his time in painting, engraving, ſinging, and driving chariots. *(i)* Philip of Macedon gave lectures on muſic; and even undertook to correct the maſters of it, which led one of them to ſay, *God forbid, Sir, that you ſhould be ſo unhappy as to underſtand this ſubject better than I do.* But Philip himſelf was ſenſible of the like impropriety in his ſon. For obſerving that Alexander had diſcovered, at an entertainment, too much ſkill in muſic, *Are you not aſhamed,* ſaid he, *that you can ſing ſo well?*

(i) Tacit. Annal. lib. 3., cap. 3.

SUETONIUS informs us, that the Emperor Tiberius uſed to enquire of the Grammarians, *Quæ mater Hecubæ; quod Achillis nomen inter Virgines fuit; quid Sirenes cantare ſint ſolitæ?*

well? *(k)* Marcus Antoninus expreffes his thankfulnefs to the Gods, that they had not fuffered him to make any great proficiency in the arts of eloquence and poetry, left he fhould have been tempted to neglect the more effential qualifications of his imperial office. And Tacitus, fpeaking of his father in law Agricola, obferves with applaufe, that he retained his moderation even in the purfuit of knowledge. *Retinuit quod eft difficillimum, ex fapientia modum. (l)*

The BIGOT and VISIONARY.

EUDOXUS was a country clergyman of learning and education: But he had early contracted a tafte for controverfial divinity; and as he devoted himfelf to ftudy, and feldom mixed with the world, his imagination became inflamed with the ideal importance of certain fpeculative

E 3 points

points of religion, which were the objects
of his unremitting attention. He had
compofed an elaborate treatife to prove
that Jefus Chrift, after his crucifixion,
actually defcended into hell ; and as his
work was ready for the Prefs, he wanted
only a patron, to whom it might be dedi-
cated. The refpectable character of the
Earl of --------, whofe amiable virtues
conciliate the love and efteem of all who
have the honour to be known to him, foon
determined his choice; and putting his
manufcript in his pocket, he fet out without delay to vifit this excellent nobleman.
" His Lordfhip, faid he to himfelf, will
doubtlefs think that I pay a very high
compliment to him, by placing his name
at the head of a book, in which I have obtained fuch a glorious victory over the
daring adverfaries of the moft important
doctrine of our holy church. The laurels
with which my brow will be crowned,
cannot fail to add new luftre to the
Mæcenas whom I have chofen. And
he will with gratitude repay, by fome
fubftantial

fubftantial emolument, the literary dignity which I fhall now confer upon him.
My Lord's perfonal intereft is great at
Court; and his Grace the Duke of --------
will fecond the recommendation of me,
with all his influence. I may therefore
fecurely depend upon the immediate gift
of a rich benefice. Perhaps one of the
golden Prebends of Durham, may now be
vacant; but my eye is fixed on the Chan-
cellorfhip of the diocefe of Chefter: And
though the worthy Doctor, who fills that
high office, enjoys a found conftitution,
and good health, from his great temperance, chearfulnefs, and equanimity, yet
he is far advanced in years, and will, ere
long, pay the common debt to nature.
This preferment will foon lead me to a
Bifhopric; and I fhall then be able to
accomplifh the great fcheme of reformation,
which I have long projected. The King,
who is a good Chriftian, muft *hate* all
Arians and Socinians; and he will heartily
concur with me in purging the church of
herefy and fchifm." Such were the flat-

tering

tering reveries, which occupied the mind of Eudoxus, whilft he was journeying towards the feat of his noble patron. His road lay over the foreft of Delamere; but being loft in thought he had given the reins to his horfe, which carried him, by taking a wrong path, to the centre of this dreary folitude. Here he found himfelf, when he awaked from the dreams of his imagination. The night was coming on; a ftorm was gathering in the horizon; the fheep-tracks fo interfected each other, that he knew not how to direct his courfe; and he wandered for fome time in the moft diftreffing perplexity. At length the cloud which threatened him, burft over his head; and he haftened, for fhelter from the rain, to a ruinous hovel, which he faw at no great diftance. Fatigued both in mind and body, he fecured his horfe, and laid himfelf on the ground. The hollow wind whiftled around him, and by its lulling influence, balmy fleep, the fweet reftorer of nature, ftole upon his clofing eye-lids. At day-break he arofe to encounter frefh for-

rows

rows and difafters. The firft objeét which
he faw was a goat tearing into pieces his
laboured manufcript. The mifchievous
animal had taken refuge, in the night,
under the fame tottering roof which fhel-
tered him; and whilft he lay afleep had
picked the papers out of his pocket. Eudoxus flew to ftop the ravages of this barbarous Goth; and colleéting his fcattered
fragments, more precious than the leaves
of the Sybils, he endeavoured to put them
again into order. But it was impoffible;
fo mangled were the fheets, and the writing
fo much effaced by the rain. He had no
other copy of his work; and he bewailed
aloud his own difappointment, and the
irreparable lofs which the world had fuftained. His plaintive and elevated voice
drew to the fide of the hovel a fhepherd,
who was going at this early hour to unfold
the flocks which he tended. Eudoxus, in
an agony of paffion, cried out to him,
Your goat has undone me; he has deftroyed my vindication of our Saviour's defcent
into *Hades*. — The honeft fhepherd was a
ftranger

ftranger to the fubject; but he faw a
Gentleman in diftrefs, whofe apparel be-
fpoke him to be of a profeffion, which he
had been juftly taught to refpect. With
a generous hofpitality, he offered him a
fhare of the homely provifions which his
wallet contained; and he conducted him,
feveral miles over the foreft, into the great
road which leads to Northwich. In this
place Eudoxus ftaid awhile to recruit his
ftrength and fpirits; and then fet out on
his return home, where he long indulged,
in fecret, his vexation and forrow.

THE fpeculative doctrines of religion, as
they have no influence on the moral conduct of mankind, are comparatively of
little importance. They cannot be underftood by the generality even of chriftians;
and the wife, the learned, and the good
have in all ages differed, and will ever
continue to differ about them. An intemperate zeal, therefore, for fuch points
of faith, betrays a weak underftanding and
contracted heart: And that zeal may juftly
be

be deemed intemperate which exceeds the value of its object; and which abates our benevolence towards thofe who do not adopt the fame opinions with ourfelves. The religion of Chrift breathes the moft generous and charitable fpirit, bringing with it *peace on earth, and good will to men.* And at the folemn day of judgment, our Saviour defcribes himfelf as demanding of the trembling finner, not of what church are you a member? or what creeds have you acknowledged? But have you fed the hungry? have you cloathed the naked? have you vifited the fick? have you improved thofe talents which the Deity has beftowed upon you to increafe your own felicity, by promoting that of your fellow creatures?

> For modes of faith let angry Zealots fight,
> His can't be *damn'd* whofe life is in the right.

EUDOXUS is an example of the folly and odioufnefs of pride. The pride of wealth is contemptible; the pride of learning is pitiable; the pride of dignity and rank is
ridiculous;

ridiculous ; but the pride of bigotry is infupportable.   No man of common fpirit will fuffer another to arrogate to himfelf dominion over his faith and confcience.

The bigot is generally a man of warm and violent paffions. He is therefore likely to be vifionary in his fchemes, and fanguine in his purfuits.   And when the mind is occupied by one great object, a thoufand leffer circumftances, which are neceffary to the attainment of it, are overlooked and neglected.   Hence arife the frequent difappointments which occur in the world ; efpecially to men of afpiring views, or of great ardour in bufinefs.

PERSECUTION.

LORD Herbert of Cherbury relates, that when he was at Paris, Father Segnerand, Confeffor to the King of France, preached a fermon before his Majefty on the chriftian duty of *forgiving our enemies*.

But

But he made a diftinction in the objects of forgivenefs, afferting that we are bound only to forgive *our perfonal* enemies, not the enemies of *God*: Such are heretics, and particularly the Profeffors of the Proteftant Religion. Thefe he urged his Majefty, as the moft *Chriftian King*, to extirpate, wherever they were to be found.

FALSE NOTIONS of PROVIDENCE.

" HOW *providential* is the rain," cried the exulting farmer, who had gathered into his barns a large crop of hay, whilft his neighbours were yet in the midft of that harveft ? " The change of weather will foon fill my meadows with grafs; and my cattle may now riot in the plenty of autumnal and winter food, which Heaven, with peculiar indulgence, has provided for them."----

SIMILAR to this is the language of the felfifh and contracted mind, on every

profperous

profperous incident of life. The partial interpofition of fovereign wifdom and power is prefumed, without hefitation; and we have the folly and vanity to believe that the order of nature is difturbed, for our benefit, even on the flighteft occafions. Whatever foundation there may be, in reafon or fcripture, for the doctrine of a *particular Providence*; the common application of it is equally abfurd and irreligious. It argues pride and arrogance in man; and difparages the moral character of the great Parent of the univerfe.

CRUELTY in EXPERIMENTS.

EUPHRONIUS was happy whenever the engagements of his profeffion, and his duty as a parent, allowed him a leifure hour to devote to experimental philofophy. He had been long purfuing a moft interefting train of inquiries into the nature and properties of various kinds of air, in concert with his learned friend

Dr.

Dr. Prieftley. And he had juft prepared, for a particular purpofe, fome mephitic water *(m)*, which was ftanding by him in a glafs veffel, when Alexis came haftily into his ftudy with a number of fmall fifhes, that he had caught, and preferved alive. The youth knew the fatality of fixed air to animals which breathe; but he wifhed to fee its effects on the inhabitants of a different element. And Euphronius, to gratify his impatient curiofity, put the fifhes into the mephitic water; through which they darted with amazing velocity, and then dropped down lifelefs to the bottom of the veffel.

SURPRISE and joy fparkled in the eyes of Alexis.-----Beware, my fon! faid Euphronius, of obferving fpectacles of pain and mifery with delight. Cruelty, by infenfible degrees, will fteal into your heart; and every generous principle of your nature

ture

(m) WATER impregnated with fixed air, which is feparated from chalk or pot-afh by means of oil of vitriol, or any other acid.

ture will then be fubverted. The Philofopher, who has in contemplation the efta-
blifhment of fome important truth ; or the
difcovery of what will tend to the advancement of *real fcience*, and to the good and
happinefs of mankind, may perhaps be
juftified if he facrifice to his purfuits the
life or enjoyment of an inferior animal.
But the emotions of humanity fhould never
be ftifled in his breaft; his trials fhould
be made with tendernefs, repeated with
reluctance, and carried no farther than the
object in view unavoidably requires. Wanton experiments on living creatures; and
even thofe which are merely fubfervient
to the gratification of curiofity, merit the
fevereft cenfure. They degrade the man
of letters into a brute; and are fit amufements only for the Cannibals of New
Zealand. I condemn myfelf for the indulgence which I juft now fhewed you.
But I knew that your fifhes would endure
lefs pain from an inftant, than from the
lingering death which awaited them; and
I little expected that your compaffionate
and

and amiable heart could have received a
pleafurable impreffion, on fuch an occafion.

The MOUSE's PETITION,

Found in the TRAP where he had been confined
all Night.

Parcere fubjectis, et debellare fuperbos.
VIRGIL.

OH! hear a penfive captive's prayer,
   For liberty that fighs;
And never let thine heart be fhut
   Againft the prifoner's cries.

For here forlorn and fad l fit,
   Within the wiry grate;
And tremble at th' approaching morn,
   Which brings impending fate.

If e'er thy breaft with freedom glow'd,
   And fpurn'd a tyrant's chain,
Let not thy ftrong oppreffive force
   A free-born moufe detain.

Oh!

Oh ! do not ſtain with guiltleſs blood
 Thy hoſpitable hearth ;
Nor triumph that thy wiles betray'd
 A prize ſo little worth.

The ſcatter'd gleanings of a feaſt
 My ſcanty meals ſupply ;
But if thine unrelenting heart
 That ſlender boon deny,

The chearful light, the vital air,
 Are.bleſſings widely given ;
Let nature's commoners enjoy
 The common gifts of Heaven.

The well-taught philoſophic mind
 To all compaſſion gives ;
Caſts round the world an equal eye,
 And feels for all that lives.

If mind, as ancient ſages taught,
 A never-dying flame,
Still ſhifts thro' matter's varying forms,
 In every form the ſame,

Beware, leſt in the worm you cruſh
 A brother's ſoul you find ;
And tremble, leſt thy luckleſs hand
 Diſlodge a kindred mind.

Or,

Or, if this tranfient gleam of day
  Be *all* of life we fhare,
Let pity plead within thy breaft
  That little *all* to fpare.

So may thy hofpitable board
  With health and peace be crown'd ;
And every charm of heartfelt eafe
  Beneath thy roof be found.

So when unfeen deftruction lurks,
  Which men like mice may fhare,
May fome kind angel clear thy path,
  And break the hidden fnare.
                        MRS. BARBAULD.

FOPPERY.

SUETONIUS *(n)* relates, that a young
officer, to whom Vefpafian had given
a commiffion, *perfumed* himfelf when he
went to Court, to thank the Emperor for
the honour which he had conferred upon
him. *I fhould have been lefs offended if you
had fmelled of garlick,* faid Vefpafian, who
              F 2   was

(n) Sueton. lib. 8.

was fo difgufted with his foppery, that he immediately difmiffed him from his poft.

SLANDER.

EUPHRONIUS heard, with indignation, the character of a much refpected
friend traduced. But he calmed the painful
emotions of his mind, by the recollection
of Mr. Pope's obfervation, that

> Envy does Merit as its fhade purfue,
> And like the fhadow, proves the fubftance true.

To flatter ourfelves with univerfal applaufe, is an inconfiftency in our expectations, dictated by folly, and foftered by
felf-love. The generality of mankind are
influenced by a *levelling principle*, which
cannot brook fuperior excellence ; and
they wage fecret war with whatever rifes
above their own mediocrity, as a kind of
moral or intellectual ufurpation. When
Ariftides, fo remarkable for his inviolable
attachment

attachment to juftice, was tried by Oftra-
cifm, (o) at Athens, and condemned to
banifhment, a peafant who could not write,
and who was unacquainted with his perfon,
applied to him to put the name of Ariftides
upon his fhell. " Has he done you any
" wrong, faid Ariftides, that you are for
" punifhing him in this manner ?" " No,
" replied the country man, I don't even
" know him ; but I am tired and angry
" with hearing every one call him *the Juft*."
Ariftides, without farther expoftulation,
calmly took the fhell, wrote upon it his
own condemnation, and returned it to the
peafant. (p)

But independent of the pride and envy
of mankind, there are few public virtues
which, from their own nature, can be
exercifed without giving umbrage. The
upright magiftrate, who hears with im-
F 3   partiality,

(o) A form of trial, in which the people of Athens voted
a perfon's banifhment, by writing his name on a fhell, which
was caft into an urn.

(p) Plut. in Arift. p. 322, 323.

partiality, and decides with wifdom and
equity, creates an enemy in the *oppreffor*,
when he redreffes the wrongs of the *oppreffed*.
The benevolent citizen, who purfues with
zeal and fteadinefs the good of the community, muft facrifice to the important
objects which he has in view, the interfering
interefts of many individuals, who will
indulge aloud their complaints, and pour
upon him a torrent of abufe. And the
liberal man, whofe hand is ever ftretched
forth to relieve ficknefs, poverty, and
diftrefs; and who diffufes happinefs around
him, by his generofity, hofpitality, and
charity, is calumniated by the worthlefs,
who partake not of his bounty; and cen-
fured even by his beneficiaries, becaufe his
kindnefs falls fhort of their unreafonable
expectations. Louis the Fourteenth ufed
to fay, that whenever he beftowed a vacant
employment, he made a hundred perfons
difcontented, and one ungrateful. The love
of liberty, civil and religious, is odious to
the tyrant, the bigot, and the *paffive* flave.
Reproof, however delicate, feafonable, and
affec-

affectionate, too often creates averfion to the friend who adminifters it. Counfel, if it contradict our darling paffion, though wife and prudent, will produce ill will. Courage excites fear and hatred in the coward. Induftry bears away the palm of fuccefs from the flothful. And learning, judgment and fkill afford advantages which irritate, becaufe they humiliate the ftupid and the ignorant. The immortal Harvey, in one of his letters to a friend, complains that he had hurt his intereft as a phyfician, by the difcovery of the circulation of the blood; a difcovery which does honour to phyfic, to philofophy, and to human nature, becaufe it was the refult, not of accident, but of folid reafoning and patient inquiry.

It is evident therefore that, in the prefent conftitution of things, envy and detraction are the price which muft be paid for pre-eminence in virtue. The fcriptures denounce woe upon thofe of whom all men fpeak well. Such characters cannot

F 4   be

be more than negatively good; and they
are generally much below the common
ftandard of merit. The vulgar phrafe of
approbation, which we fo frequently hear
applied to the individuals of this clafs,
that they are enemies to no one but themfelves,
conveys the fevereft fatyr; becaufe it implies that they are either infignificant
drones, grofs hypocrites, or the infamous
panders of pleafure. Tully defcribes CA-
TALINE himfelf as popular, by having the
artifice *cum triftibus feverè, cum remiffis ju-*
cundè, cum fenibus gravitèr, cum juventute
comiter vivere; that is, by fervilely accom-
modating himfelf to the humours and
vices of all with whom he converfed.

ARE we then to regard *fame* as unattainable, or as unworthy of a wife man's
purfuit? Certainly not. Such a conviction
would fupprefs a noble and powerful incitement to virtue, and deftroy one of the
moft exquifite enjoyments of human life.
For the pleafure arifing from the applaufes
of the judicious and the good, is next, in
degree

degree, to the inward delight which flows from the confcioufnefs of having deferved them. And he who governs by reafon this animating principle of action; who uniformly aims at moral rectitude in his conduct; who fuffers not popular praife or vulgar opinion to elate or to miflead him; and who is undepreffed by the cenfures of interefted or incompetent judges, *(q)* will command the efteem and love of thofe, whofe fuffrages alone are fame; will be honoured and revered by pofterity; and will obtain the favour of God himfelf, the omnifcient obferver and fovereign rewarder of merit.

PRAISE WHEN YOU MAY;
BE CANDID WHEN YOU CAN.

SEVERAL Gentlemen, in the company of Lord Bolingbroke, were fpeaking of the avarice of the Duke of Marlborough;
and

(q) Falfus honor juvat, et mendax infamia terret,
Quem, nifi mendacem, & mendofum ? ---

and they appealed to his Lordſhip for the
truth of the inſtances which they produced. " He was ſo great a man, replied
Lord Bolingbroke, that I have forgotten
his vices." — A truly generous anſwer for
a political enemy to make! The Duke
and Lord Bolingbroke were of oppoſite
parties.

VOLTAIRE.

CIRCUMSPECTION.

LUCY and Emilia were admiring the
ſtructure of a ſpider's web, which
was formed between the branches of a tall
ſhrub, in the garden at Hart-Hill; when
Euphronius, returning from his morning
walk, ſtopped to inquire what object ſo
much engaged their attention, The dew-
drops yet beſpangled the fine threads, of
which the web was compoſed, and rendered every part of it conſpicuouſly beautiful.
A ſmall winged inſect happened, at this
inſtant, to be caught in the toil; and the
ſpider,

spider, before invisible, advanced along
the lines from his secret retreat, seized the
prey, and killed it by instilling a venomous
juice into the wound he made. When the
rapacious tyrant had almost devoured his
game, another fly, of a larger size, became
entangled in the mesh. He now waited
patiently till the insect was fatigued, by
struggling to obtain its liberty; and then
rolling the web around it, he left the poor
fly in a state of terror and impotence, as a
future repast for his returning appetite.

You pity the fate, said Euphronius, of
this unfortunate insect, whose destruction
is the natural consequence of its ignorance
and want of caution. Remember that you
yourselves will be exposed, in the commerce of life, to various snares, dangerous
to your virtue, and subversive of your peace
of mind. FLATTERY is the common *toil*
laid for your sex; and when you are entangled in it, vanity, affectation, pertness,
and impatience of controul constitute the
poison which is then infused into your
wounded

wounded bofoms. PLEASURE fpreads a glit-
tering *web*, which has proved fatal to
thoufands.   AMBITION *catches* the unwary
by power, titles, dignities, and prefer-
ments.   And FALSE RELIGION, under a
dazzling outfide of myfterious fanctity, and
pompous ceremonies, conceals a *net work*
of prieftcraft and fuperftition, from which
it will be ftill more difficult to extricate
yourfelves.   Sophron and Alexis had now
joined the little party; and Euphronius,
pointing to them his difcourfe, bid them
beware of the Cobwebs of PHILOSOPHY;
thofe fine fpun *hypothefes*, which involve
the mind in error, and unfit it for the patient inveftigation of truth by obfervation
and experiment. -------- Here the moralift
was interrupted by a fervant, who came to
inform him that his carriage waited at the
door.

THE WEAKNESS OF MAN, AND THE WISDOM OF DIVINE PROVIDENCE.

DISORDERS of the intellect occur
much more frequently than fuperficial
obfervers

obfervers will eafily believe. There is no man whofe imagination does not fome-times predominate over his reafon; and every fuch tyranny of fancy is a temporary degree of infanity. He who delights in filent fpeculation, often indulges, without reftraint, the airy vifions of the foul, and expatiates in boundlefs futurity; amufing his defires with impoffible enjoyments, and conferring upon his pride unattainable do-minion. In time fome particular train of ideas abforb the attention; the mind recurs conftantly, in wearinefs or leifure, to the favourite conception; and the fway of fan-cy becomes defpotic. Delufions then ope-rate as realities; falfe opinions engrofs the underftanding; and life paffes in dreams of pleafure or of mifery.

An Egyptian aftronomer, who had fpent forty years in unwearied attention to the motions and appearances of the heavenly bodies, conceived that he was invefted with the power of regulating the weather, and varying the feafons. The fun, he
thought,

thought, obeyed his mandates, and paſſed
from tropic to tropic by his direction.
The clouds burſt at his call on the ſouth-
ern mountains ; and the inundations of
the Nile were governed by his will. He
mitigated the rage of the Dog ſtar ; reſtrained the equinoctial tempeſts ; and diſ-
penſed rain and ſun-ſhine to the ſeveral
nations of the earth. *(r)* Such power,
though imaginary, was too extenſive for
the feebleneſs of man ; and the aſtronomer
ſunk under the burthens of an office,
which he laboured to adminiſter with impartial juſtice, and univerſal benevolence.
The diſcordant claims of different regions
and climates ; and the oppoſite requiſitions
of the various fruits of the ground in the
ſame

(r) So far is borrowed, with conſiderable variations, from
Raſſelas, Prince of Abyſſinia, a novel written by Dr. Samuel
Johnſon. The original affords a ſtriking picture of literary
inſanity ; but the imaginary powers of the aſtronomer, over
the univerſe, are confined to the diſtribution of rain and ſun-
ſhine. He is repreſented alſo as equal, in his own idea, to the
government of nature ; and anxious only for a proper ſucceſſor.
I have given a different turn to the narration, with a view to
convey more important inſtruction to the mind.

fame diftrict, haraffed his mind with in-
ceffant care, fufpenfe, and perplexity. If
he fuffered the clouds to pour down their
treafures on the thirfty defarts of Arabia,
impetuous torrents overwhelmed the fertile
plains of Baffora. And when he fent forth
a ftorm, to fweep away the peftilential
Samiel, *(s)* which carried death and defo-
lation in its progrefs, a fleet, laden with
the richeft merchandife, was fhipwrecked
in the gulf of Ormus. The fervid beams
of the fun, whilft they matured the lufcious
grape of Smyrna, deftroyed the harveft of
corn, and fcorched the herbage of the
fields. The philofopher thought he could
perhaps remedy thefe evils, by turning
afide the axis of the earth, and varying the
ecliptic of the fun. But he found it impoffible to make a change of pofition, by
which

(s) THE Samiel is a fudden vapour, to which travellers
are expofed in the defarts of Arabia, in the months of June,
July, and Auguft. It brings inftantaneous death to every
man or beaft, that happens to ftand in the way of it. This
peftiferous guft quickly paffes, and does not extend itfelf far;
but runs, as it were, in ftreams of no great breadth.

Vid, Mr. Ives' Journal.

which the world could be advantaged.
And he dreaded the injury, which he might
occafion, to diftant and unknown parts of
the folar fyftem.　Oppreffed with anxiety,
he earneftly folicited the great Governor
of the univerfe to diveft him of the painful
pre-eminence, with which he was honoured.　" Father of light, he cried, thy omnipotent hand, and all-feeing eye are alone
equal to the mighty empire of this globe.
The vaft operations of nature exceed my
finite comprehenfion ;　and I now feel,
with reverence and humility, that to dif-
penfe good and evil in all thofe varied
combinations, which conftitute the harmo-
nious fyftem on which the general happinefs depends, nothing lefs can be required
than unerring wifdom, fpotlefs rectitude,
and fovereign power."

THE Deity liftened with indulgence to a
prayer which flowed from a fincere and
pious heart : In the folly of the aftronomer
he faw and pitied the weaknefs of human
nature ; and by ftrengthening the prefent
conviction

conviction of his mind, he gracioufly removed the infanity under which he laboured.

THE CHARACTER OF THE MERCHANT
HONOURABLE.

YOU live in a mercantile country, my
fon, and I wifh you to think refpect-
fully of the character of a merchant. Hear
the fentiments of the firft genius of the
age on this fubject. " In France, fays
Voltaire, the title of Marquis is given
gratis to any one who will accept of it ;
and whofoever arrives at Paris, from the
moft remote province, with money in his
purfe, and a name terminating in *ac* or *ille*,
may ftrut about, and cry, Such a man as
I ! a man of my rank and figure ! and may
look down upon a trader with fovereign
contempt : whilft the trader on the other
fide, by thus often hearing his profeffion
treated fo difdainfully, is fool enough to
blufh at it. However, I need not fay

G   which

which is moſt uſeful to a nation; a lord powdered in the tip of the mode, who knows exactly at what o'clock the king riſes and goes to bed, and who gives him-ſelf airs of grandeur and ſtate, at the ſame time that he is acting the ſlave in the anti-chamber of a prime miniſter; or a mer-chant, who enriches his country, diſ-patches orders from his compting-houſe to Surat and Grand Cairo, and contributes to the felicity of the world."

A FEMALE CHARACTER.

HER kindly melting heart,
    To every want and every woe,
To guilt itſelf when in diſtreſs,
The balm of pity would impart,
And all relief that bounty could beſtow !
Ev'n for the kid or lamb that poured its life
        Beneath the bloody knife,
        Her gentle tears would fall,
As ſhe the common mother were of all.

    Nor only good, and kind,
But ſtrong and elevated was her mind :
A ſpirit that with noble pride
        Could look ſuperior down,
        On Fortune's ſmile, or frown ;

That

That could without regret or pain
To virtue's loweſt duty facrifice,
Or intereſt's, or ambition's higheſt prize;
That injur'd or offended never try'd
Its dignity by vengeance to maintain,
But by magnanimous diſdain.

A wit, that temperately bright
With inoffenſive light
All pleaſing ſhone, nor ever paſt
The decent bounds that Wiſdom's ſober hand
And ſweet Benevolence's mild command,
And baſhful modeſty, before it caſt.
A prudence undeceiving, undeceiv'd
That nor too little, nor too much believ'd,
That ſcorn'd unjuſt Suſpicion's coward fear,
And without weakneſs knew to be ſincere.

LORD LYTTELTON,

CRUELTY to HORSES.

IN the month of June, Lucy, Emilia,
and Jacobus were carried by Hortenſia
to view the crouds of company, as they
paſſed to the races, which are annually
held upon Kerſal Moor near Mancheſter.
The variety of countenances which they

G 2 ſaw;

faw; the mirth of fome, the eagernefs
of others, and the diffipation of all, furnifhed a delightful entertainment to their
young minds, unalloyed by any reflections
on the extravagance, gaming, and intemperance which fuch diverfions produce.
Whilft they were enjoying this fcene of
pleafure, they obferved two men advancing on a full gallop, fpurring and
lafhing their horfes to increafe their fpeed.
The day was extremely hot, and one of
the horfes fell gafping almoft at the feet of
Jacobus. By his agility the rider inftantly
freed himfelf from the ftirrups, and rifing
with fury from the ground, he beat his
horfe in the moft favage and relentlefs
manner. The poor animal was unable to
move; and at every ftroke of the whip expreffed his agonies by the moft piercing
groans. In vain the furrounding croud
interceded in his behalf. The tyrant to
whom he belonged, inflamed with anger
and revenge, continued inexorable; and
Hortenfia withdrew, with her young charge,
from a fpectacle fo painful and diftreffing.

WHEN

WHEN Euphronius returned to Hart-Hill in the evening, his children flocked around him, impatient to relate this tale of woe. I know and pity the unhappy horfe, faid he; and if you will liften to me, I will give you the particulars of his hiftory. The fire of this animal was a native of Arabia felix, where he ranged without controul in the moft fertile and extenfive plains, enjoying all the luxuries of nature. He was the leader of a herd which confifted of more than five hundred of his fpecies; and thus fupported by the united force of numbers, no beaft of the foreft durft attack him. When his followers flept he ftood as centinel, to give notice of approaching danger; and if an Arab happened to advance, he fometimes walked up boldly towards him, as if to examine his ftrength, or to intimidate him; then inftantly he gave the fignal to his fellows, by a loud fnorting, and the whole herd fled with the fwiftnefs of the wind. In one of thefe flights he was taken by a trap, concealed upon the ground, which

G 3   entangling

entangling his feet, made him an eafy prey
to the hunter. He was carried to Con-
ftantinople; fold to the Britifh envoy
there; and brought by him into England,
to improve our breed of horfes. The firft
colt he got, was the poor animal whofe
fufferings you now lament, and whom I
remember to have feen gay, frolicfome,
and happy. He was fed in a large pafture,
where he ufed to gallop round and round;
trying every active movement of his limbs,
and increafing his ftrength and agility by
thofe gambols and exercifes which jocund
nature, in early youth, infpires. Thus
paffed the firft period of his life; but now
his ftate of fervitude and mifery commenced. To render him more tame and paffive, a painful operation was performed
upon him, by which the fize and firmnefs
of his mufcles were impaired, his fpirit
was depreffed, and he loft, with the diftinction of his fex, one effential power of
ufefulnefs and enjoyment. Nature had
furnifhed him with a flowing tail, which
was at once an ornament, a covering for
                                    what

what fhould be concealed, and a weapon
of defence againft the flies of fummer.
But falfe tafte decreed the extirpation of
it; and feveral joints were taken off by a
coarfe inftrument, and blundering farrier.
The blood gufhed from the wound; and
to ftop the difcharge, the tender part was
feared with a red hot iron. At this inftant
of time I happened to pafs by; and whilft
I was pierced to the heart with the fufferings of the horfe, I faw the favage who
inflicted them, fufpend his operation, to
curfe and beat him for the groans he uttered. When the tail was thus reduced to
a ridiculous fhortnefs, it was thought that a
turn upwards would give additional grace
to it. And to produce this effect, feveral
deep cuts were made on the under fide
of it; and the tail was drawn by a cord
and pulley into a moft painful pofition,
till the granulation of the flefh was compleated. He was now trained, or broken,
as it is ufually termed, for riding; and
during this feafon of difcipline, he under-
went all the feverities of the lafh and the

G 4   fpur.

fpur.   Many a time were his fides covered
with blood, before his averfion to the afs
could be fully fubdued.   The dread of
this animal he derived from his fire ; for
in the ftate of nature, the afs and the horfe
bear the utmoft antipathy to each other.
And if a horfe happen to ftray into the
paftures where the wild affes graze, they
attack him with fury ; and furrounding
him to prevent his flight, they bite and
kick him till he dies.   When rendered
perfectly tractable, he was fold to the prefent proprietor, whom he has faithfully
and affectionately ferved during ten years.
He has been a companion to him in various journeys ; has borne him with eafe and
fecurity many thoufand miles ; has contri-
buted to reftore him from ficknefs to health,
by the gentle exercife which he afforded ;
and by the fwiftnefs of his feet he has
twice refcued him from robbers and affaf-
fins.   But he is now growing old ; his
joints become ftiff ; his wind fails him ;
and urged beyond his fpeed, on fo fultry a
day, he fell breathlefs at your feet.   In a
few

few hours he recovered himfelf; and the owner has fince difpofed of him, at a low price, to the mafter of the poft horfes in Manchefter. He is now to be ridden as a common hackney, or to be driven in a chaife; and he will be at the mercy of every coxcomb traveller, who *gallops* night and day through different countries, to acquire a knowledge of mankind, by the obfervation of their manners, cuftoms, laws, arts, police, and government. It is obvious that the horfe will foon be difqualified for this violent and cruel fervice; and if he furvive, he will be fold to grind in a mill. In this fituation his exercife will be lefs fevere, but almoft without intermiffion; the movement in a circle will produce a dizzinefs of the head; and in a month or two he will become blind. Still, however, his labours are to continue; and he may drag on years of toil and forrow, ere death clofes the period of his fufferings.

THE children were much affected by this narrative;

narrative; and Jacobus cried out, with
emotion, " I love my little horfe, and
" will never abufe him. And when he
" grows old, he fhall reft from his work;
" and I will feed him, and take care of
" him till he dies."

POSITIVENESS.

THE Cameleon is a fmall quadruped,
in fhape refembling a Crocodile,
and chiefly found in Arabia and Egypt. It
is a vulgar error that this animal feeds
upon air; for his ftomach is always found
to contain flies and other infects. Mr. Le
Bruyn, during his abode at Smyrna, had
four Cameleons in his poffeffion. He never
perceived that they eat any thing, except
now and then a fly. Their colour often
changed, without any apparent caufe; but
their moft durable one was grey, or rather
a pale moufe colour. Sometimes the
animals were of a beautiful green, fpotted
with yellow; at other times they were
marked

marked all over with dark brown; but he never found that they affumed a red colour. Thefe properties of the Cameleon have given rife to the following fable, which was written by Mr. Merrick, and fhews, in a lively and ftriking manner, the folly of pofitivenefs in opinion.

THE CAMELEON.

OFT has it been my lot to mark
   A proud, conceited, talking fpark,
With eyes, that hardly ferv'd at moft
To guard their mafter 'gainft a poft,
Yet round the world the blade has been
To fee whatever could be feen,
Returning from his finifh'd tour,
Grown ten times perter than before;
Whatever word you chance to drop,
The travell'd fool your mouth will ftop,
" Sir, if my judgment you'll allow—
" I've feen—and fure I ought to know"—
So begs you'd pay a due fubmiffion,
And acquiefce in his decifion.

   Two travellers of fuch a caft,
As o'er Arabia's wilds they paft,
And on their way in friendly chat
Now talk'd of this, and then of that,

Difcours'd

Difcours'd awhile 'mongft other matter,
Of the Cameleon's form and nature.
" A ftranger animal, cries one,
" Sure never liv'd beneath the fun :
" A lizard's body lean and long,
" A fifh's head, a ferpent's tongue,
" Its tooth with triple claw disjoin'd ;
" And what a length of tail behind !
" How flow its pace ! and then its hue—
" Who ever faw fo fine a blue ? "

" Hold there, the other quick replies,
" Tis green — I faw it with thefe eyes,
" As late with open mouth it lay,
" And warm'd it in the funny ray ;
" Stretch'd at its eafe the beaft I view'd,
" And faw it eat the air for food.

" I've feen it, Sir, as well as you,
" And muft again affirm it blue.
" At leifure I the beaft furvey'd
" Extended in the cooling fhade."

" 'Tis green, 'tis green, Sir, I affure ye—
" Green ! cries the other in a fury —
" Why, Sir—d'ye think I've loft my eyes ? "
" 'Twere no great lofs, the friend replies,
" For, if they always ferve you thus,
" You'll find 'em but of little ufe."

So

So high at laſt the conteſt roſe,
From words they almoſt came to blows;
When luckily came by a third —
To him the queſtion they referr'd;
And begg'd he'd tell 'em, if he knew,
Whether the thing was green or blue.

" Sirs, cries the umpire, ceaſe your pother —
" The creature's neither one nor t'other.
" I caught the animal laſt night,
" And view'd it o'er by candle light :
" I mark'd it well — 'twas black as jet —
" You ſtare — but Sirs, I've got it yet,
" And can produce it."—" Pray, Sir, do :
" I'll lay my life the thing is blue."
" And I'll be ſworn, that when you've ſeen
" The reptile, you'll pronounce him green."

" Well then, at once to eaſe the doubt,
" Replies the man, I'll turn him out :
" And when before your eyes I've ſet him,
" If you don't find him black, I'll eat him."
He ſaid : then full before their ſight
Produc'd the beaſt ; and lo ! 'twas white. —
            DODSLEY'S COLLECTION, Vol. V.

LYING.

MENDACULUS was a youth of good
parts, and of amiable diſpoſitions;
but

but by keeping bad company he had contracted, in an extreme degree, the odious
habit of lying. His word was fcarcely
ever believed by his friends ; and he was
often fufpected of faults, becaufe he denied
the commiffion of them, and punifhed for
offences, of which he was convicted only
by his affertions of innocence. The experience of every day manifefted the dif-
advantages which he fuffered from the
habitual violation of truth. He had a
garden ftocked with the choiceft flowers ;
and the cultivation of it was his favourite
amufement. It happened that the cattle of
the adjoining pafture had broken down the
fence ; and he found them trampling upon,
and deftroying a bed of fine auriculas. He
could not drive thefe ravagers away, without endangering the ftill more valuable
productions of the next parterre ; and he
haftened to requeft the affiftance of the
gardener. " You intend to make a fool
of me," faid the man, who refufed to go,
as he gave no credit to the relation of
Mendaculus.

ONE

ONE frosty day, his father had the misfortune to be thrown from his horse, and to fracture his thigh. Mendaculus was present, and was deeply affected by the accident, but had not strength to afford the necessary help. He was therefore obliged to leave him, in this painful condition, on the ground, which was at that time covered with snow; and, with all the expedition in his power, he rode to Manchester, to solicit the aid of the first benevolent person he should meet with. His character as a liar was generally known; few to whom he applied paid attention to his story; and no one believed it. After losing much time in fruitless entreaties, he returned with a sorrowful heart, and with his eyes bathed in tears, to the place where the accident happened. But his father was removed from thence: A coach fortunately passed that way; he was taken into it, and conveyed to his own house, whither Mendaculus soon followed him.

A LUSTY

A LUSTY boy, of whom Mendaculus
had told fome falfhoods, often way-laid
him as he went to fchool, and beat him
with great feverity. Confcious of his ill
defert, Mendaculus bore, for fome time,
in filence this chaftifement; but the frequent repetition of it at laft overpowered
his refolution, and he complained to his
father of the ufage which he met with.
His father, though dubious of the truth of
this account, applied to the parents of the
boy who abufed him. But he could obtain no redrefs from them, and only received the following painful anfwer: "Your
fon is a notorious liar, and we pay no regard to his affertions." Mendaculus was
therefore obliged to fubmit to the wonted
correction, till full fatisfaction had been
taken by his antagonift for the injury
which he had fuftained.

SUCH were the evils in which this unfortunate youth almoft daily involved himfelf, by the habit of lying. He was fenfible of his mifconduct, and began to reflect
upon

upon it with ferioufnefs and contrition.
Refolutions of amendment fucceeded to
penitence; he fet a guard upon his words;
fpoke little, and always with caution and
referve; and he foon found, by fweet
experience, that truth is more eafy and
natural than falfhood. By degrees the love
of it became predominant in his mind;
and fo facred at length did he hold veracity
to be, that he fcrupled even the leaft
jocular violation of it. This happy change
reftored him to the efteem of his friends;
the confidence of the public; and the peace
of his own confcience.

VIGILANT OBSERVATION.

BE attentive, my dear Alexis, to every
event which occurs, and to all the
objects which furround you. Suffer nothing to efcape your notice. The minuteft
fubftance, or the moft trivial incident may
furnifh important knowledge, or be applied
to fome ufeful purpofe. I have heard that

H   the

the great law of gravitation, by which the whole fyftem of the univerfe is governed, was firft fuggefted to the mind of Sir Ifaac Newton by the accidental fall of an apple, which he obferved on a very ftill day, in a garden. Archimedes, a Sicilian Philofo-pher who flourifhed about two centuries before Chrift, happened to remark whilft he was bathing, that the bulk of the water was increafed, in a certain proportion, by the immerfion of his body. A fortunate train of ideas inftantly arofe in his mind ; he faw at one view the method of afcertain-ing the fpecific gravities of bodies, that is, how much they are lighter or heavier than others of a different kind ; and he perceived that he fhould now be able to detect the fraud of an artift, who had mixed bafe metal with the gold of King Hiero's crown. So overjoyed was he at this difcovery, that, it is faid, he ran naked out of the bath into the ftreets of Syracufe, crying out, "I have found it ! I have found it !" The hydro-ftatical balance is framed on the theorem of Archimedes, *that a body heavier than*

water

water weighs lefs in water than in air, by the weight of as much water as is equal to it in bulk. And this inftrument is employed to eftimate the purity of metals, the richnefs of ores, and the relation which a variety of fubftances bear to each other.

DR. FRANKLIN, when he was on board the fleet of fhips bound againft Louifbourg in 1757, happened to obferve that the wakes of two of the veffels were remarkably fmooth, whilft thofe of all the reft were ruffled by the wind, which then blew frefh. He was puzzled with the appearance, and pointing it out to the captain of his fhip, afked him the caufe of it. " The cooks, faid he, have probably been pouring out their greafy water." Though this folution by no means fatisfied the Philofopher, he determined to take the firft opportunity of trying the effect of oil on water. And you are well acquainted with the fuccefs of his curious and very ufeful experiments on this fubject.

WE

We are informed by Mr. Boyle, that Harvey had the firſt glimpſe of the circulation of the blood, from a view of the valves of the veins, as they were exhibited by Fabricius the anatomiſt, to his pupils. The invention of Mezzotintos is ſaid to have taken riſe from the obſervance of regular figures on a ruſty gun-barrel. Geoffroy relates that the virtues of the Peruvian bark were diſcovered by an Indian, who in the hot fit of an intermittent, drank largely of the water of a pool, into which ſome of thoſe trees, that yield it, had fallen. ——But I ſhall repeat no farther inſtances of this kind, till I can add to the number ſome valuable acquiſition of yours; the happy fruit, my dear Alexis, of your ſagacity and attention.

PASSION.

TWO Gentlemen were riding together, one of whom, who was very choleric, happened

happened to be mounted on a high-mettled horfe. The horfe grew a little trouble-fome, at which the rider became very angry, and whipped and fpurred him with great fury. The horfe, almoft as wrong-headed as his mafter, returned his treat-ment by kicking and plunging. The companion, concerned for the danger, and afhamed of the folly of his friend, faid to him coolly, *Be quiet, be quiet, and fhew yourfelf the wifer of the two.*

THE WORLD, Vol. IV.

FAMILY LOVE AND HARMONY.

I WILL amufe you with a little experi-ment, faid Sophron, one evening, to Lucy, Emilia, Alexis and Jacobus; and rifing from the table, he took the candles and held them about half an inch afunder, oppofite to a medallion of Dr. Franklin, *(t)*

H 3 and

(t) Made by the author's very ingenious friends Meffrs. Wedgwood and Bentley; whofe improvements in the fine arts do honour to this age and nation.

and about two yards diftant from it. The
motto round the figure, UNHURT AMIDST
THE WAR OF ELEMENTS, was juft diftinctly
vifible. When the degree of light had
been fufficiently obferved, he united the
flames of the two candles, by putting them
clofe together; and the whole figure, with
the infcription, became inftantly illumina-
ted in a much ftronger manner than before.
They were all pleafed and ftruck with the
effect; and they defired Euphronius, who
now entered the parlour, to explain to them
the caufe of it. He commended their entertainment, and informed them, that a
greater degree of *heat* is produced by the
junction of the two flames, and confequent-
ly a farther attenuation and more copious
emiffion of the particles, of which light
confifts. But, my dear children, continued he, attend to the leffon of *virtue* as
well as of *fcience*, which the experiment
you have feen affords. Nature has im-
planted in your hearts benevolence, friendfhip, gratitude, humanity, and generofity;
and thefe focial affections are feparately

fhining

ſhining lights in the world. But they burn
with peculiar warmth and luſtre, when more
concentred in the kindred charities of brother, ſiſter, child, and parent. And harmony, peace, ſympathy in joy and grief, mutual
good offices, forgiveneſs, and forbearance,
are the bright emanations of domeſtic love.
Oh! may the radiance of ſuch virtues long
illuminate this happy houſhold!

A

FATHER's INSTRUCTIONS;

CONSISTING OF

MORAL TALES, FABLES,

AND

REFLECTIONS.

PART THE SECOND.

QUOD MUNUS REIPUBLICÆ AFFERRE MAJUS
MELIUSVE POSSUMUS, QUAM SI DOCEMUS AT-
QUE ERUDIMUS JUVENTUTEM.

CICERO.

TO

THE MEMORY OF

THE RIGHT HONOURABLE

H U G H,

LORD WILLOUGHBY OF PARHAM;

CHAIRMAN OF THE COMMITTEES

OF THE HOUSE OF PEERS;

PRESIDENT OF THE SOCIETY OF ANTIQUARIES;

VICE PRESIDENT OF THE ROYAL SOCIETY;

AND OF THE

SOCIETY FOR THE ENCOURAGEMENT OF ARTS;

A TRUSTEE OF THE BRITISH MUSEUM;

AND

ONE OF THE COMMISSIONERS OF LONGITUDE;

A NOBLEMAN,

WHO UNITED IN HIS CHARACTER,

THE WISDOM OF THE SENATOR,

WITH THE LEARNING OF THE PHILOSOPHER;

THE TALENTS FOR ACTIVE,

AND THE VIRTUES OF CONTEMPLATIVE LIFE;

THIS TRIBUTE

OF

VENERATION, GRATITUDE, AND AFFECTION,

DUE TO A LAMENTED

COUNSELLOR, BENEFACTOR, AND FRIEND,

IS INSCRIBED

BY

THE AUTHOR.

T O

T. B. P.—A. P.—F. P.—J. P.
G. B. P. &c. &c.

My Dear Children,

THROUGH the indulgence
of a kind Providence, I
am again permitted to dedicate
the effusions of a tender heart,
to your improvement; and I am
persuaded that you will receive
them with pleasure and respect,
as the counsels of a faithful
friend, and affectionate father.
Harsh reproof and stern authority you have never experienced.
Love has been the motive; and
reason,

reafon, fince you were capable
of being governed by it, the rule
of your obedience. And each
revolving year has added to your
virtues, and to my felicity. Soon,
however, the connection in
which we now rejoice, will be
diffolved. The frequent inter-
ruptions of my health, and the
natural delicacy of my conftitution, warn me of the precarious
tenure, on which I hold the
deareft bleffings of life ; and
heighten my attachment to you,
and to my friends, whilft they
render me indifferent to almoft
every other enjoyment. It is our
wifdom therefore, and I truft it

is

is our mutual wifh, to improve
the fleeting period of our union ;
to cherifh the generous fympathies, which the filial and paternal relations infpire ; and to difcharge our reciprocal duties with
affiduity, delight, and perfeverance.

In thefe pages I fhall continue
to addrefs you, with a Father's
fond folicitude, when my tongue
hath loft its utterance, and my
heart hath ceafed to feel. Nor
will you be deaf to my inftructions, though the voice be heard
no more, which once delivered
them. With pious tendernefs
you

you will recollect the love from which they flowed ; and gratitude will confer on them a value, far beyond their humble claim of merit.

Such are the pleasing expectations I have formed ; and which your amiable dispositions, and affectionate behaviour fully justify. Oh! may no clouds arise, to obscure the brightness of the prospect now before me! May wisdom and virtue, more and more illuminate your path! And at the close of life, may it be my honour and felicity, to have supported the endearing character

ter of your guardian, friend, and father ! Adieu.

THOMAS PERCIVAL.

MANCHESTER,
Jan. 1ft. 1777.

Advertisement.

THE Instructions of a Father to his Children have been received with candour and indulgence by the public; and the Author submits, without reluctance, the continuation of his work, to the same impartial tribunal. Paternal affection first suggested the plan; experience hath evinced its utility; and both conspire to encourage the prosecution of it.

THIS volume, like the former, is adapted to very different ages and occasions. The moral tales and reflections it contains, are addressed to the hearts and understandings of a numerous young family; for whose future, as well as present improvement, they have been composed.

MORAL

TALES, FABLES,

AND

REFLECTIONS.

Habes a patre munus, Marce fili ; fed perinde erit, ut acceperis.——His voluminibus ad te profecta vox mea eft ; tribues his temporis quantum poteris ; poteris autem, quantum voles.——Tibi perfuade te mihi quidem effe cariffimum ; fed multo fore cariorem, fi talibus monumentis praceptifque latabere.

CICERO.

M O R A L

T A L E S,   F A B L E S,

A N D

R E F L E C T I O N S.

The true ENJOYMENTS of LIFE.

MAY he survive his relatives and friends! was the imprecation of a Roman, on the perfon who fhould deftroy the monument of his anceftors*(a)*. A more dreadful curfe could fcarcely be denounced. I remember to have feen it fomewhere recorded,

I 3

ed,

(a) Quisquis. Hoc. Sustulerit.
aut. Jusserit.
Ultimus. Suorum. Moriatur.
Fleetwood Infcript. Antiq. p. 221.

ed, that an Emperor of China, on his ac-
ceffion to the throne, commanded a general
releafe from the prifons, of all that were
confined for debt. Amongft the number
was an old man, who had been an early
victim to adverfity; and whofe days of
imprifonment, reckoned by the notches
which he had cut on the door of his
gloomy cell, expreffed the annual revolu-
tion of more than fifty funs. With faulter-
ing fteps, he departed from his manfion of
forrow: His eyes were dazzled with the
fplendor of light; and the face of nature
prefented to his view a perfect paradife.
The jail, in which he had been imprifoned,
was at fome diftance from Pekin; and he
directed his courfe to that city, impatient
to enjoy the gratulations of his wife, his
children, and his friends.

WITH difficulty he found his way to the
ftreet, in which formerly ftood his decent
habitation; and his heart became more
and more elated at every ftep which he
advanced. He proceeded, and looked
with earneftnefs around; but faw few of
                                        thofe

thofe objects with which he was formerly converfant. A magnificent edifice was erected on the fite of the houfe which he had inhabited. The dwellings of his neighbours had affumed new forms; and he beheld not a fingle face of which he had the leaft recollection. An aged pauper, who ftood with trembling knees at the gate of a portico, from which he had been thruft by the infolent menial who guarded it, ftruck his attention. He ftopped to give him a pittance out of the bounty, with which he had been fupplied by the Emperor's liberality; and received, in return, the fad tidings that his wife had fallen a lingering facrifice to penury and forrow; that his children were gone to feek their fortunes in unknown climes; and that the grave contained his neareft and moft valuable friends. Overwhelmed with anguifh, he haftened to the palace of his Sovereign, into whofe prefence his hoary locks and mournful vifage foon obtained admiffion; and cafting himfelf at the feet of the Emperor, Great Prince, he cried, remand me to the prifon, from which miftaken mercy

I 4   hath

hath delivered me! I have furvived my family and friends; and in the midft of this populous city, I find myfelf in dreary folitude. The cell of my dungeon protected me from the gazers at my wretchednefs; and whilft fecluded from fociety, I was lefs fenfible of the lofs of focial enjoyments. I am now tortured with the view of pleafures in which I cannot participate; and die with thirft, though ftreams of delight furround me.

If the horrors of a dungeon, my Alexis, be preferred to the world at large, by the man who is bereft of his kindred and friends, how highly fhould you prize, how tenderly fhould you love, and how ftudious fhould you be to pleafe thofe near and dear relations, whom a more indulgent Providence has yet preferved to you! Liften to the affectionate counfels of your parents; treafure up their precepts; refpect their riper judgment; and enjoy, with gratitude and delight, the advantages refulting from their fociety. Bind to your bofom, by the moft endearing ties, your brothers and
fifters;

fifters; cherifh them as your beft companions, through the variegated journey of life;
and fuffer no jealoufies or feuds to interrupt
the harmony which now reigns, and, I
truft, will ever reign in this happy family.
Cultivate the friendfhip of your father's
friends; merit the approbation of the wife
and good; qualify yourfelf, by the acquifition of knowledge and the exercife of the
benevolent affections, for the intercourfe of
mankind; and you will at once be an ornament to fociety, and derive from it the
higheft felicity.

A WINTER EVENING's CONVERSATION.

THE family of Euphronius had left
their retirement at Hart-Hill, where

" Dead the vegetable kingdom lay,
" And dumb the tuneful."

THOMSON.

His fire-fide at Manchefter was furrounded
by a young and fmiling circle; and the
various labours and incidents of the day
furnifhed

furnifhed topics of amufing converfation for the evening. Each, in fucceffion, was the little hero of his own important tale; and Sophron clofed the entertainment, by repeating the Geographical Leffon which he had learned, and recounting his travels over the terraqueous globe.

ALL liftened with eager attention to the wondrous narration. He told them of the orange groves, and fpicy woods of Weftern and Eaftern India; defcribed the gold and filver mines of Peru, the rich diamonds of Brazil and of Bengal, and the ivory tufks of the Elephant, found in the forefts of Africa. In artlefs colours, he painted the dreary regions and eternal fnows of the Northern and Southern Poles; and when a general chill had feized his fympathetic audience, he prefented to their aftonifhed view the louds of fmoke, and torrents of liquid fire difcharged by Hecla, Vefuvius, and Ætna. Thefe impreffions of horror were for awhile fufpended, when he dif-played the vaft expanfe of the ocean, un-ruffled by a breath of wind, reflecting every

where

where the azure fky, and crowded with myriads of fportive fifhes. But a ftorm fucceeds; the fwelling billows mount into the heavens, the fhattered bark is borne aloft on the fummit of a wave, and then hurled into the gulph below, where fhe is dafhed againft a treacherous rock, or fwallowed by the horrible abyfs.

SOPHRON proceeded to the hiftory of animated nature: He pictured the Lion which inhabits the burning defarts of Zaara; pointed out the juft proportions of his make, in which ftrength is united with agility, his undaunted look, and tremendous roar, refembling diftant thunder. The peaceable Rhinoceros, that provokes not to combat, yet difdains to fly, even from the monarch of the foreft; the fierce Tyger, the favage and untameable Hyena, and the artful Crocodile, were each defcribed. Nor did he forget the Camel, patient of hunger and thirft; the monftrous Hippopotamos, found in the rivers Nile, and Niger; and the Ouran-Outang, fo near in its approaches to the human form. The
fcaly

fcaly tribe of fifhes he barely noticed; but dwelt longer on the ftructure, properties, and habitudes of the feathered race. He particularly enlarged on the fongfters of the wood, who delight the eye, and charm the ear, by their varied plumage, and enchanting notes. Thefe pleafing notes, he faid, like human language, are not *innate (b)*; but depend on the *imitation* of fuch founds, as the birds moft frequently hear, and which their organs are adapted to perform. A young Robin has been taught the fong of the Nightingale; and a Linnet, which belonged to Mr. Matthews at Kenfington, almoft articulated the words *pretty boy*. The common Sparrow, taken from the neft when juft fledged, and educated with the Goldfinch and the Linnet, acquires the mufic of each; and the powers of the mocking bird are expreffed by its very name. Canary birds, which are fo much admired in this country, are imported from Tyrol, where the Nightingale was originally employed as their inftructor

in

(b) Philofophical Tranfactions, Vol. 63. p. 249.

in finging. The traffic in thefe birds forms
an article of commerce, as four Tyrolefe
generally bring over to England fixteen
hundred every year. And though they
carry them one thoufand miles by land,
and pay a duty of twenty pounds for this
number, yet they reap a fufficient profit
from the fale of them *(c)*.

HERE Sophron concluded the hiftory of
his travels, of which this is only a brief
relation. Alexis, Lucy, Emilia, and Jacobus continued in mute attention, ex-
pecting further wonders; and the looks of
Euphronius expreffed the fatisfaction which
he felt. You have given us, faid he to
Sophron, a lively and juft defcription of
the globe, its productions, and brute inhabitants: But Man, who, by the fuperiority of his mental powers, is the lord of
the creation, and whofe nature and character form the moft interefting and important objects of inquiry, has been overlooked in your furvey. Climate, foil, laws,
cuftoms,

(c) Philolopnical Tranfactions, Vol. 63. p. 261.

cuftoms, food, and other accidental dif-
ferences have produced an aftonifhing variety in the complexion, features, manners,
and faculties of the human fpecies. The
moft refined and polifhed nations may be
diftinguifhed from each other; and a river
is fometimes the only boundary between
two favage tribes, who are as diffimilar in
the tincture of their fkin, as in the difpofition of their minds. But all mankind have
one common ftructure; all are formed with
the powers of reafon, with the moral affections, and with a capacity for happinefs.
The varieties amongft the human race, e-
numerated by Linnæus and Buffon, are fix.
The firft is found under the polar regions,
and comprehends the Laplanders, the
Efquimaux Indians, the Samoeid Tartars,
the inhabitants of Nova Zembla, the Bo-
randians, the Greenlanders, and the people
of Kamtfchatka. The vifage of men, in
thefe countries, is large and broad; the
nofe flat and fhort; the eyes of a yellowifh
brown, inclining to blacknefs; the cheek
bones extremely high; the mouth large;
the lips thick, and turned outwards; the
voice

voice thin and fqueaking; and the fkin of a dark grey colour(d). The people are fhort in ftature, the generality being about four feet high, and the talleft not more than five. Ignorance, ftupidity and fuper-ftition are the mental characteriftics of the inhabitants of thefe rigorous climates. For here

" Doze the grofs race. Nor fprightly jeft nor fong,
" Nor tendernefs they know, nor aught of life,
" Beyond the kindred bears that ftalk without."(e)

THE Tartar race, under which may be comprehended the Chinefe, and the Japa-nefe, forms the fecond great variety in the human fpecies. Their countenances are broad and wrinkled, even in youth; their nofes fhort and flat; their eyes little, funk in the fockets, and feveral inches afunder; their cheek bones are high; their teeth of a large fize, and feparate from each other; their complexions olive-coloured; and their hair black. Thefe nations, in gene-ral, have no religion, no fettled notions of morality,

(d) Krantz. Goldfmith's Hiftory of the Earth.
(e) Thomfon's Seafons.

morality, and no decency of behaviour.
They are chiefly robbers; their weälth
confifts in horfes, and their fkill in the
management of them.

THE third variety of mankind is that of
the fouthern Afiatics, or the inhabitants of
India. Thefe are of a flender fhape, have
long ftraight black hair, and generally
Roman nofes. Their complexions are of
an olive colour, and in fome parts, quite
black. Thefe people are flothful, luxurious, fubmiffive, cowardly, and effemi-
nate *(f)*.

—— The parent Sun himfelf
Seems o'er this world of flaves to tyrannize;
And with oppreffive ray, the rofeate bloom
Of beauty blafting, gives the gloomy hue,
And feature grofs : or worfe, to ruthlefs deeds,
Mad jealoufy, blind rage, and fell revenge,
Their fervid fpirit fires.   Love dwells not there,
The foft regards, the tendernefs of life,
The heart fhed tear, th' ineffable delight
Of fweet humanity: thefe court the beam

Of

(f) See Goldfmith's Hiftory of the Earth.

Of milder climes ; in felfifh fierce defire,
And the wild fury of voluptuous fenfe,
There loft. The very brute creation there
This rage partakes, and burns with horrid fire. *(g)*

THE Negroes of Africa conftitute the fourth ftriking variety in the human fpecies : But they differ widely from each other; thofe of Guinea, for inftance, are extremely ugly, and have an infupportably offenfive fcent; whilft thofe of Mofambique are reckoned beautiful, and are untainted with any difagreeable fmell. The Negroes are, in general, of a black colour; and the downy foftnefs of the hair, which grows upon their fkin, gives a fmoothnefs to it, refembling that of velvet. The hair of their heads is woolly, fhort, and black; but their beards often turn grey, and fometimes white. Their nofes are flat and fhort, their lips thick and tumid, and their teeth of an ivory whitenefs *(h)*.

THE intellectual and moral powers of
K   thefe

(g) Thomfon's Summer.
(h) See Goldfmith's Hiftory of the Earth.

these wretched people are uncultivated; and they are subject to the most barbarous despotism. The savage tyrants, who rule over them, make war upon each other for *human plunder*; and the wretched victims, bartered for spirituous liquors, or the wares of Birmingham and Manchester, are torn from their families, their friends, and native land, and consigned for life to misery, toil, and bondage *(i)*. But how am I shocked to inform you, that this infernal commerce is carried on by the humane, the polished, the christian inhabitants of Europe; nay even by Englishmen, whose ancestors have bled in the cause of liberty, and whose breasts still glow with the same generous flame! I cannot give you a more striking proof of the ideas of horror, which the captive negroes entertain of the state of servitude they are to undergo, than by relating the following incident from Dr. Goldsmith.

(i) It appears from the most accurate calculations, says Abbe Raynal, that a seventh part of the Blacks, imported from the coast of Guinea, die every year. Fourteen hundred thousand unhappy beinge, who are now in the European colonies in the new world, are the unfortunate remains of nine millions of slaves who have been conveyed thither.

Goldfmith. "A Guinea Captain was, by
ftrefs of weather, driven into a certain
harbour, with a lading of very fickly
flaves, who took every opportunity to
throw themfelves over-board, when brought
upon deck for the benefit of the frefh air.
The Captain perceiving, amongft others,
a female flave attempting to drown herfelf,
pitched upon her as a proper example for
the reft. As he fuppofed that they did not
know the terrors attending death, he ordered the woman to be tied with a rope
under the arm-pits, and fo let down into
the water. When the poor creature was
thus plunged in, and about half way down,
fhe was heard to give a terrible fhriek,
which at firft was afcribed to her fears of
drowning; but foon after, the water ap-
pearing red around her, fhe was drawn up,
and it was found that a Shark, which had
followed the fhip, had bitten her off from
the middle." *(k)*

K 2   THE

(k) The practice of domeftic flavery prevailed in the moft
polifhed ages of the Greeks and Romans, and had a very per-
nioious influence on the manners of thofe nations. It is related
that

THE native inhabitants of America make a fifth race of men. They are of a copper colour, have black, thick, ftraight hair, flat nofes, high cheek bones, and fmall eyes. They paint the body and face of various colours, and eradicate the hair of their beards and of other parts, as a deformity. Their limbs are not fo large and robuft, as thofe of the Europeans. They endure hunger, thirft, and pain with aftonifhing firmnefs and patience; and, though cruel to their enemies, they are kind and juft to each other.

THE Europeans may be confidered as the laft variety of the human kind. But it is unneceffary to enumerate the perfonal marks which diftinguifh them, as every day affords you opportunities of making fuch obfervations. I fhall only fuggeft to you, that they enjoy fingular advantages

from

that Vedius Pollio, in the prefence of Auguftus, ordered one of his flaves, who had committed a flight offence, to be cut in pieces and thrown into the fifh pond, to feed his fifhes. But the Emperor, with indignation, commanded him inftantly to emancipate that flave, and all the others who belonged to him.

from the fairnefs of their complexions.
The face of the African Black, or of the
olive-coloured Afiatic, is a very imperfect
index of the mind, and preferves the fame
fettled fhade in joy and forrow, confidence
and fhame, anger and defpair, ficknefs and
health. The Englifh are faid to be the
faireft of the Europeans, and we may
therefore prefume, that their countenances
beft exprefs the variations of the paffions,
and the viciffitudes of difeafe. But the
intellectual and moral characteriftics of the
different nations, which compofe this quarter of the globe, are of more importance
to be known. Thefe however become
gradually lefs difcernible, as fafhion, learning, and commerce prevail more univerfally; and I fhall leave them, as objects of
your future inquiry.

Thus paffed a winter evening by the
fire-fide of Euphronius, whofe pleafing,
though anxious tafk it was,

" To rear the tender thought;
" To teach the young idea how to fhoot;
" To pour the frefh inftruction o'er the mind;

" To

" To breathe th' enlivening ſpirit ; and to fix
" The generous purpoſe in the glowing breaſt." *(l)*

SISTERLY UNITY AND LOVE.

OBSERVE thoſe two hounds that are coupled together, ſaid Euphronius to Lucy and Emilia, who were looking through the window. How they torment each other, by a diſagreement in their purſuits ! One is for moving ſlowly, and the other vainly urges onward. The larger dog now ſees ſome object that tempts him on this ſide, and mark how he drags his companion along, who is exerting all his efforts to purſue a different rout ! Thus they will continue all day at variance, pulling each other in oppoſite directions, when they might, by kind and mutual compliances, paſs on eaſily, merrily, and happily *(m)*.

LUCY

(l) Thomſon's Seaſons.

(m) I am indebted to Mr. Dodſley for the ſubject, but not for the narration or moral application of this fable.

Lucy and Emilia concurred in cenfuring the folly and ill-nature of thefe dogs; and Euphronius expreffed a tender wifh, that he might never fee any thing fimilar in their behaviour to each other. Nature has linked you together, by the near equality of age; by your common relation to the moft indulgent parents; by the endearing ties of fifterhood; and by all thofe generous fympathies, which have been foftered in your bofoms from your earlieft infancy. Let thefe filken cords of mutual love continue to unite you in the fame purfuits. Suffer no allurements to draw you different ways; no contradictory paffions to diftract your friendfhip; nor any felfifh views or fordid jealoufies to render thofe bonds uneafy and oppreffive, which are now your ornament, your ftrength, and higheft happinefs.

An APPEARANCE in NATURE explained, AND IMPROVED.

ONE morning, in the month of September, as Alexis was riding with

Euphronius

Euphronius from Hart-Hill to Manchefter,
he noticed, with furprife, the fudden difperfion of a thick fog, which had obfcured
every object around them.   The fun now
fhone in full fplendour; and the veil being
withdrawn from the face of nature, the
hills and dales, the meadows, corn-fields,
and woodlands feemed to meet the eye
with renewed beauty and luftre.   As foon
as they were arrived in town, Euphronius
took a glafs of *clear* fpring water, and
threw into it a teafpoonful of falt.   An
opacity almoft inftantly enfued through the
whole of it; but when the glafs was placed
near the fire, and gently agitated, the
liquor quickly recovered its tranfparency.
This experiment, faid Euphronius to his
fon, explains to you the phænomenon you
lately obferved.   The watery vapours,
floating in the atmofphere, which formed
the thick mift we found fo incommodious
to us, were diffolved by the air, as foon as
the fun had given fufficient warmth and
motion to its particles: And in the evening, the fog will again return, and the
dews defcend, from the abfence of that
genial

genial influence, which now diffolves and renders them invifible. This glafs of falt and water, which has been withdrawn from the fire, as it becomes colder, lofes, in the fame manner, its tranfparency. Does your amiable heart, my dear Alexis, fuggeft to you any other analogy? There are mifts of the mind as well as of the atmofphere; and the fun of reafon, like the great luminary of our fyftem, has the happy power of producing their difperfion. Religion too offers her chearing *light*, when the foul is clouded with adverfity, and overfpread with gloom. A well grounded conviction that all events are under the direction of Providence, and a firm reliance on the power, wifdom, and goodnefs of the Deity, will difpel every anxious thought; illuminate and extend into futurity our profpects; and, by contrafting brightnefs with fhades, will beautify the chequered landfcape of life.

The HISTORY of JOSEPH ABRIDGED.

ISRAEL loved Jofeph more than all his children, becaufe he was the fon of his old age; and he gave him a coat of many colours. But when his brethren faw their father's partiality to him, they hated him, and would not fpeak peaceably unto him. And Jofeph dreamed a dream, and he told it to his brethren. Behold, he faid, we were binding fheaves in the field, and lo, my fheaf arofe and ftood upright, and your fheaves ftood round about, and made obeifance to my fheaf. And his brethren faid unto him, Shalt thou indeed have dominion over us? And they hated him the more for his dreams and for his words.

It happened that his brethren went to feed their father's flock in Dothan. And Jofeph went after his brethren; but when they faw him afar off, they confpired againft him to flay him, and they faid one to another, We will tell our father that

fome

fome evil beaft hath devoured him. But
Reuben wifhed to deliver him out of their
hands, and he faid, Let us not kill him,
but caft him into this pit, that is in the
wildernefs. And they followed his counfel, and caft him into the pit, which then
contained no water. A company of Ifhmaelites from Gilead paffed by at this time,
with their camels, bearing fpicery, balm,
and myrrh, which they were carrying into
Egypt. And Judah faid unto his brethren,
Let us fell Jofeph to the Ifhmaelites, and
let not our hands be upon him, for he is
our brother and our flefh : And Jofeph was
fold for twenty pieces of filver. And his
brethren killed a kid, and dipt his coat in
the blood thereof. And they brought it
unto their father, and faid, This have we
found. And Jacob knew it, and believing
that Jofeph was devoured by an evil beaft,
he rent his cloaths, and put fackcloth on
his loins, and refufed all comfort, faying, I
will go down into the grave to my fon,
mourning. Thus wept his father for him.
But Jofeph was carried into Egypt and fold
to Potiphar, the captain of Pharaoh's
guard.

guard. And the Lord was with him, and profpered him, and he found favour in the fight of his mafter. But by the wickednefs of Potiphar's wife, he was caft into the prifon, where the king's prifoners were bound. Here alfo the Lord continued to fhew him mercy, and gave him favour in the fight of the keeper of the prifon. And all the prifoners were committed to his care, amongft whom were two of Pharaoh's officers, the chief of the butlers and the chief of the bakers. And Jofeph interpreted the dreams of the king's fervants, and his interpretation being true, the chief butler recommended him to Pharaoh, who had dreamed a dream, which Jofeph thus fhewed unto him. Behold there fhall come feven years of great plenty, throughout all the land of Egypt: And there fhall arife, after them, feven years of famine, and all the plenty fhall be forgotten in the land of Egypt, and the famine fhall confume the land.

AND the King faid unto Jofeph, Forafmuch as God hath fhewn thee all this, thou

thou fhalt be over mine houfe, and according to thy word fhall all my people be ruled. And Jofeph gathered up all the food of the feven years, and laid up the food in ftorehoufes. Then the feven years of dearth began to come, as Jofeph had foretold. But in all the land of Egypt there was bread, and people from all countries came unto Jofeph to buy corn, becaufe the famine was fore in all the lands. Now amongft thofe that came, were the ten fons of Jacob, from the land of Canaan. And Jofeph faw his brethren, and he knew them, but made himfelf ftrange unto them, and fpoke roughly to them, faying, "Ye are fpies." And they faid, Thy fervants are twelve brethren, the fons of one man in the land of Canaan; and behold the youngeft is this day with our father, and one is not.

But Jofeph faid unto them, Ye fhall not go forth hence, except your youngeft brother come hither. Let one of your brethren be bound in prifon, and go ye to carry corn for the famine of your houfes,

and

and bring your youngeſt brother unto me.
And their conſciences reproached them,
and they ſaid one to another, We are
verily guilty concerning our brother, in
that we ſaw the anguiſh of his ſoul, when
he beſought us, and we would not hear;
therefore is this diſtreſs come upon us.
And they knew not that Joſeph underſtood
them, for he ſpake unto them by an inter-
preter.   And he turned himſelf about
from them, and wept; and returned to
them again, and communed with them;
and took from them Simeon, and bound
him before their eyes.   And they returned
unto Jacob their father, in the land of
Canaan, and told him all that had befallen them.   And Jacob, their father,
ſaid unto them, " Me have ye bereaved of
my children: Joſeph is not, and Simeon
is not, and ye will take Benjamin away
alſo.   But my ſon ſhall not go down with
you, for his brother is dead, and he is left
alone: If miſchief befal him in the way in
which ye go, then ſhall ye bring down
my grey hairs with ſorrow to the grave."
But the famine continued ſore in the land;
and

and when they had eaten up the corn, which they had brought out of Egypt, Jacob faid unto them, Go again, and buy us food. And if it muft be fo, now take alfo your brother Benjamin, and arife and go unto the man. And they brought prefents unto Jofeph, and bowed themfelves to him to the earth, And he afked them of their welfare, and faid, Is your father well? Is he alive? And he lifted up his eyes, and faw Benjamin his brother; and his bowels did yearn towards his brother; and he fought where to weep, and he entered his chamber and wept there. And he wafhed his face, and went out, and refrained himfelf. Then he commanded the fteward of his houfe, faying, Fill the men's facks with food, as much as they can carry, and put my cup, the filver cup, into the fack of Benjamin, the youngeft. And the fteward did according to the word that Jofeph had fpoken. As foon as the morning was light, the men were fent away, they and their affes. But Jofeph commanded his fteward to follow them, and to fearch their facks, and to bring

them

them back. And when Judah and his brethren were returned into the city, Jofeph faid unto them, " What deed is this that ye have done ? The man in whofe hands the cup is found fhall be my fervant; and as for you, get you in peace unto your father." But they faid, " Our father will furely die, if he feeth that the lad is not with us ; and we fhall bring down the grey hairs of thy fervant our father with forrow to the grave." Then Jofeph could not refrain himfelf before all them that ftood by him; and he cried, Caufe every man to go out from me ; and there ftood no man with him, whilft Jofeph made himfelf known unto his brethren. And he wept aloud, and faid unto his brethren ; I am Jofeph ; doth my father yet live ? And his brethren could not anfwer him, for they were troubled at his prefence. And Jofeph faid unto his brethren, Come near to me, I pray you ; and they came near : And he faid, I am Jofeph your brother, whom ye fold into E-gypt. Now therefore be not grieved, nor angry with yourfelves, that ye fold me hi-

ther ;

ther; for God did fend me before you, to
fave your lives by a great deliverance.
Hafte you, and go up to my father, and
fay unto him, Thus faith thy fon Jofeph;
God hath made me lord of all Egypt;
come down unto me, tarry not. And
thou fhalt dwell in the land of Gofhen,
and thou fhalt be near unto me, thou, and
thy children, and thy children's children,
and thy flocks, and thy herds, and all that
thou haft. And there will I nourifh thee;
for yet there are five years of famine; left
thou, and thy houfhold, and all that thou
haft, come to poverty. And behold your
eyes fee, and the eyes of my brother Benjamin, that it is my mouth which fpeaketh
unto you. And you fhall tell my father of
all my glory in Egypt, and all that you
have feen; and ye fhall hafte, and bring
down my father hither.

AND he fell upon his brother Benjamin's
neck, and wept; and Benjamin wept upon
his neck. Moreover, he kiffed all his
brethren, and wept upon them; and after
that, his brethren talked with him. And

L   the

the fame thereof was heard in Pharaoh's houſe; and it pleaſed Pharaoh well, and his ſervants. And Pharaoh ſaid unto Joſeph, Invite hither thy father, and his houſhold; and I will give them the good of the land of Egypt; and they ſhall eat the fat of the land. And the ſpirit of Jacob was revived when he heard theſe tidings; and he ſaid, My ſon is yet alive; I will go and ſee him before I die. And he took his journey, with all that he had. And Joſeph made ready his chariot, and went up to meet Iſrael, his father, to Goſhen; and preſenting himſelf unto him, he fell on his neck, and wept on his neck for ſome time. And Joſeph placed his father, and his brethren; and gave them a poſſeſſion in the land of Egypt, in the beſt of the land, as Pharaoh had commanded.

Tʜɪs intereſting ſtory contains a variety of affecting incidents; is related with the moſt beautiful ſimplicity; and furniſhes many important leſſons of inſtruction. It diſplays the miſchiefs of parental partiality;

the

the fatal effects of envy, jealousy, and dif-
cord amongst brethren; the bleffings and
honours with which virtue is rewarded;
the amiablenefs of forgiving injuries; and
the tender joys which flow from fraternal
love and filial piety. Different in other
refpects as your lot may be from that of
Jofeph, you have a father, my dear Alexis,
who feels for you all the affection which
Ifrael felt, and who hopes he has a claim
to the fame generous return of gratitude.
You have brothers and fifters, who are
ftrangers to hatred, who will cherifh and
return your love, and whofe happinefs is
infeparable from yours: And you are under the protection and authority of that
eternal Being, the God of Abraham, of
Ifaac, and of Jacob, who fees, approves,
and will exalt the virtuous *(n)*.

L 2   GOOD.

(n) In relating the hiftory of Jofeph, an incident, which
reflects the higheft honour on his character, has been omitted,
becaufe to my younger readers it admits of no explanation,
and might wound the native modefty of thofe, who are farther
advanced in years. There is a delicacy and fenfe of decency in
the mind of an ingenuous youth, which fhields him more
powerfully from feduction, than the beft leffons of morality,
or the brighteft examples of felf-government. This tender

GOOD-NATURED CREDULITY.

A Chaldean Peafant was conducting a goat to the city of Bagdat. He was mounted on an afs, and the goat followed him, with a bell fufpended from his neck. " I fhall fell thefe animals, faid he to him- " felf, for thirty pieces of filver; and with " this money I can purchafe a new turban, " and a rich veftment of taffety, which I " will tie with a fafh of purple filk. The " young damfels will then fmile more fa- " vourably upon me.; and I fhall be the " fineft man at the Mofque." Whilft the Peafant was thus anticipating in idea his future enjoyments, three artful rogues con- certed a ftratagem to plunder him of his prefent treafures. As he moved flowly along, one of them flipped off the bell from the neck of the goat, and faftening it, without being perceived, to the tail of the

afs,

fhoot of vernal life is often injured by improper culture; it fhrinks at the fuggeftion of every loofe idea; and is blafted by their frequent and unfeafonable repetition afs, carried away his booty. The man riding upon the afs, and hearing the found of the bell, continued to mufe without the leaft fufpicion of the lofs which he had fuftained. Happening however, a fhort while afterwards, to turn about his head, he difcovered, with grief and aftonifhment, that the animal was gone, which conftituted fo confiderable a part of his riches: And he inquired, with the utmoft anxiety, after his goat, of every traveller whom he met.

THE fecond rogue now accofted him, and faid, " I have juft feen in yonder fields, a man in great hafte, dragging along with him a goat." The Peafant difmounted with precipitation, and requefted the obliging ftranger to hold his afs, that he might lofe no time in overtaking the thief. He inftantly began the purfuit, and having traverfed, in vain, the courfe that was pointed out to him, he came back fatigued and breathlefs to the place from whence he fet out; where he neither found his afs, nor the deceitful informer, to whofe care

he had entrufted him. As he walked pen-
fively onwards, overwhelmed with fhame,
vexation, and difappointment, his attention
was roufed by the loud complaints and la-
mentations of a poor man, who fat by the
fide of a well. He turned out of the way
to fympathife with a brother in affliction,
recounted his own misfortunes, and inquired the caufe of that violent forrow, which
feemed to opprefs him. Alas! faid the
poor man, in the moft piteous tone of
voice, as I was refting here to drink, I
dropped into the water a cafket full of diamonds, which I was employed to carry to
the Caliph at Bagdat; and I fhall be put
to death on the fufpicion of having fecret-
ed fo valuable a treafure. Why do not you
jump into the well in fearch of the cafket,
cried the Peafant, aftonifhed at the ftupidity of his new acquaintance? Becaufe it is
deep, replied the man, and I can neither
dive nor fwim. But will you undertake
this kind office for me, and I will reward
you with thirty pieces of filver? The Peafant accepted the offer with exultation, and
whilft he was putting off his caffock, veft,

and

and flippers, poured out his foul in thankf-
givings to the holy prophet, for this providential fuccour. But the moment he
plunged into the water, in fearch of the
pretended cafket, the man, (who was one
of the three rogues that had concerted the
plan of robbing him) feized upon his garments, and bore them off in fecurity to his
comrades.

THUS, through inattention, fimplicity,
and credulity, was the unfortunate Chaldean duped of all his little poffeffions; and
he haftened back to his cottage, with no
other covering for his nakednefs, than a
tattered garment which he borrowed on
the road(*o*).

AN EASY AND INSTRUCTIVE EXPERIMENT.

IT was a clear frofty day: The fun fhone
bright, and the ground was covered
with fnow, when Euphronius invited
L 4 Alexis,

(*o*) The ftory is faid to have been written by an Arabian
author: But I have taken the liberty of deviating from the
original, and of making additions to it.

Alexis, Lucy, Emilia, and Jacobus to
affift him in a little experiment, which
he thought would contribute to their inftruction, and amufement. He took four
pieces of woollen cloth, equal in dimenfions, but of different colours; one being
black, another *blue*, a third *brown*, and a
fourth *white*: And having chofen a proper fituation, he laid them all, very near
each other, on the furface of the fnow.
In a few hours the black piece of cloth
had funk confiderably below the furface;
the blue almoft as much; the brown a
little; but the white remained precifely in
its pofition *(p)*.

Observe, faid Euphronius, how varied
is the influence of the fun's rays on different colours? They are abforbed, and
retained by the *black*; and in the piece
of cloth before us, they have produced
fuch a ftrong and durable heat, as to melt
the fnow underneath. Their effect on
blue is nearly fimilar; but they feem not
to

(p) See Franklin's Obfervations.

to penetrate the *white:* And the piece of that colour, by having no warmth communicated to it, ftill continues on the furface of the fnow.

THIS little experiment teaches you, Emilia, that white hats will afford the beft defence to your complexion; but that they fhould have dark linings, to abforb the rays of light which are reflected from the earth. You may learn from it, Alexis, that cloaths of a light colour are beft adapted to fummer, and to hot climates; that black fubftances acquire heat fooner, and retain it longer than any other; and that fruit walls, drying ftoves, &c. fhould be painted black. Other inferences I fhall leave to you the pleafure of difcovering. Allow me only to remind you, that knowledge and virtue may be juftly compared to rays of light; and that it is my warmeft wifh, and higheft ambition, that your heart and underftanding may unite the qualities of the two oppofite colours you have been contemplating. May your mind be quick in the reception, and fteady

dy in the retention of every good impreffion!   And may the luftre of your endowments be reflected on your brothers, fifters,
and friends!

The DOG.

MY Dog, the truftieft of his kind,
With gratitude inflames my mind ;
I mark his true, his faithful way,
And in my fervice, copy Tray.
GAY's FABLES.

A Water Spaniel, belonging to a neighbour, was a frequent, and always a
moft welcome gueft in the family of Euphronius.   Her placid looks, gentle manners, and affiduity to pleafe, rendered her
equally the favourite of the fervants, and
of the children.   It happened that there
was a general alarm concerning mad dogs
in Manchefter ; and to guard againft danger, Sylvia was clofely confined to her
kennel.   A week elapfed without a fingle
vifit from her ; no one knew the caufe of
her abfence, and all lamented it.   She at
length

length returned; the children flocked with joy and eagernefs around her; but they beheld her trembling, feeble, and emaciated. She crawled over the kitchen floor; looked wiftfully at Emilia; then at Jacobus; then at Lucy: Advancing a ftep forwards, fhe licked the hand of Alexis, which was ftretched forth to ftroke her, and expired at his feet, without a groan. The children at firft ftood filent, and motionlefs; a gufh of tears fucceeded; and Euphronius, though pleafed with the fenfibility they fhewed, thought it neceffary to foften the impreffion which this affecting incident produced. He endeavoured to withdraw their attention from Sylvia, by defcribing the qualities, and relating the hiftory of the fpecies at large. I am not furprifed, faid he, that you fhould lament the lofs of an animal, whom nature feems to have peculiarly formed, to be the favourite and friend of man. The beauty of his fhape, his ftrength, agility, fwiftnefs, courage, generofity, fidelity, and gratitude, command our attachment, and give him the jufteft claim to our care and protection.

In

In obedience and docility, he furpaffes
every other quadruped: and fo perfectly is
he domesticated, that Mr Buffon obferves,
he affimilates his character to that of the
family in which he lives. Amongst the
proud he is difdainful, and churlish amongst
clowns.

In Congo, Angola, and in South America, where dogs are found wild, they
unite in packs, and attack the fierceft animals of the foreft. On the fouthern coaft
of Africa, it is faid, there are dogs that
neither bark nor bite; and their flesh is
highly valued by the Negroes *(q).* The
flesh of this animal is alfo confidered as a
dainty by the Chinefe, and public shamb-
bles are erected for the fale of it. In Can-
ton particularly there is a ftreet appropriated to that purpofe; and what is very extraordinary, whenever a dog-butcher appears, all the dogs in the place purfue
him in full cry. They know their enemy,
and perfecute him as far as they are able *(r).*

THE

(q) See Brookes' Natural Hiftory.
(r) See Goldfmith's Hiftory of the Earth.

THE influence of climate, and the efforts of art, have produced many varieties in the breed of dogs. The Britifh Maftiffs were fo famous among the Romans, that their Emperors appointed an officer in this ifland, to train them for the combats of the Amphitheatre. Three of thefe were efteemed a match for a Bear, and four for a Lion. But an experiment was made in the Tower by King James the Firft, from which it appeared that three Maftiffs conquered this noble animal. Two of them were difabled in the conflict; but the third forced the Lion to feek his fafety by flight *(s)*. The Britifh Maftiffs were alfo educated for war, and were employed by the Gauls in their battles, as we learn from Strabo *(t)* Linnæus has delivered in the following terms, the natural hiftory of the Dog.

THIS animal eats flefh, and farinaceous vegetables; but not greens, His ftomach digefts

(s) See Stowe's Annals; Pennant's Zoology; Camden's Britannia.

(t) Lib. IV.

digefts bones. He ufes the tops of grafs as a vomit; and laps his drink with his tongue. His fcent is moft exquifite, when his nofe is moift: He treads lightly on his toes; fcarcely ever fweats; but when hot lolls out his tongue. He generally walks round the place on which he intends to lie down. His fenfe of hearing is very quick when afleep: He dreams. The female goes with young fixty-three days; and commonly brings from four to eight puppies at a birth. The male puppies refemble the dog; the female the bitch. He is the moft faithful of all animals; is very docible; hates ftrange dogs; fnaps at a ftone which is thrown at him; howls at certain mufical notes; and barks at ftrangers. This quadruped is rejected by the Mahometans.

RESPECT and DEFERENCE due to the AGED.

AN aged Citizen of Athens coming late into the public Theatre of that city,

fo

fo celebrated for arts and learning, found the place crowded with company, and every feat engaged. Though the fpectators were his countrymen, and moft of them young perfons, no one had the politenefs or humanity to make room for him. But when he paffed into the part which was allotted to the Lacedemonian Ambaffadors, and their attendants, they all rofe up, and accommodated the old Gentleman with the beft, and moft honourable feat amongft them. The whole company were equally furprifed, and delighted with this inftance of urbanity, and expreffed their approbation by loud plaudits. "*The Athenians per-* "*fectly well underftand the rules of good* "*manners ;*" faid one of the Ambaffadors in return for this compliment; "*but the Lacedemonians practife them.*"

CICERO.

GAMING.

GAMING. *(u)*

THAT the love of gaming has its
foundation in avarice, is an undoubt-
ed truth; but it proceeds from a fpecies of
covetoufnefs, differing from every other.
Salluft, in his charaĉter of Cataline, has
given us an exaĉt definition of it; *Alieni
appetens, fui profufus; Profufe of his own,
greedy of the property of another.* The deftructive confequences of this vice will be
evinced by the melancholy hiftory of Lyfander. This unfortunate youth was the
only fon of Hortenfius, a gentleman of
large fortune; who with a paternal eye
watched over his education, and fuffered
no means to be negleĉted, which might
promote his future ufefulnefs, honour, or
happinefs. Under fuch tuition, he grew
up improving in every amiable accomplifh-
ment. His perfon was graceful, and his
countenance the piĉture of his foul, lively,
fweet,

(u) This is a juvenile produĉtion, written when the author
was at fchool.

fweet, and penetrating. By his own application, and the affiftance of fuitable pre-
ceptors, he was mafter of the whole circle
of fciences; and there was nothing now
wanting, to form the complete gentleman,
but travelling. The tour of Europe was
therefore refolved upon, and a proper perfon provided to attend him. Lyfander
and his tutor accordingly fet out. I pafs
over in filence the fad parting of the good
old Gentleman and his beloved fon. The
fcene may be conceived, but cannot be expreffed. Hortenfius however had this
confolation, that Lyfander was likely to
reap every advantage from fuch a temporary feparation. Our travellers directed
their courfe to France; and croffed the fea
at Dover, with an intention to pay their
firft vifit to Paris. Here Lyfander had
difficulties to furmount, of which he was
little apprifed: He had been bred up in
fhades and folitude, and had no idea of
the active fcenes of life. It is eafy to imagine therefore his furprife at being tranfported, as it were, into a new world. He
was delighted with the elegance of the

M   city,

city, and the crowds of company that reforted to the public walks. He launched
into pleafures; and was enabled to commit
a thoufand extravagances by the ample
fupplies of money which a fond father allowed him. In vain his tutor reprefented
to him the imprudence of his conduct:
captivated with the novelty of every thing
around him, he was deaf to all his remonftrances. He engaged in an intrigue with
a woman of the moft infamous character;
who in a fhort time reduced him to the
neceffity of making frefh demands upon his
father. The indulgent Hortenfius, with
a few reprimands for his profufion, and
admonitions to œconomy, remitted him
confiderable fums. But thefe were not
fufficient to fatisfy an avaricious miftrefs;
and afhamed to expofe himfelf a fecond
time to his father, he had recourfe to fortune. He daily frequented the gaming
tables; and elated with a trifling fuccefs at
the beginning, gave up every other pleafure for that of rattling the dice. Sharpers
were now his only companions, and his
youth and inexperience made him an eafy

prey

prey to their artifice and defigns. His father heard of his conduct with inexprefli-
ble forrow. He inftantly recalled him
home; but alas! the return to his native
country did not reftore him to his natural
difpofitions. The love of learning, generofity, humanity, and every noble principle were fuppreffed; and in their place
the moft deteftable avarice had taken root.
The reproofs of a father, fo affectionate as
Hortenfius, were too gentle to reclaim one
confirmed in vicious habits. He ftill purfued the fame unhappy courfe, and at
length, by his diffolute behaviour, put an
end to the life of the tendereft of parents.
The death of Hortenfius had at firft a happy effect upon the mind of Lyfander; and
by recalling him to a fenfe of reflection,
gave fome room to hope for reformation.
To confirm the good refolutions he had
formed, his friends urged him to marry.
The propofal not being difagreeable to
him, he paid his addreffes to Afpafia, a
lady poffeffed of beauty, virtue and the
fweeteft difpofitions. So many charms
could not but imprefs a heart, which filial

grief had already in fome meafure foftened.
He loved and married her; and by her
prudent conduct, was prevailed upon to
give up all the former affociates of his favourite vice. Two years paffed in this
happy manner, during which time Afpafia
bleffed him with a fon. The little darling
had united in him all *the father's luftre and
the mother's grace.* Lyfander often viewed
him with ftreaming eyes of tendernefs,
and he would fometimes cry out, " Only,
" my fon, avoid thy father's fteps, and
" every felicity will attend thee." About
this time it happened that fome bufinefs of
importance required his prefence in Lon-
don. There he unfortunately met with
the bafe wretches who had been his old acquaintance : And his too eafy temper
complying with their folicitations, again
he plunged into the abyfs of vice and folly.
Afpafia, wondering at the long abfence of
her hufband, began to entertain the moft
uneafy apprehenfions for him. She wrote
him a tender and endearing letter; but no
anfwer was returned. Full of terror and
anxiety, fhe went in perfon to inquire after
her

her Lyfander. Long was it before fhe
heard the leaft tidings of him. At length,
by accident, finding his lodgings, fhe flew
to his chamber, with the moft impatient
joy, to embrace a long loft hufband. But
ah! who can paint the agony fhe felt at
the fight of Lyfander weltering in his gore,
with a piftol clenched in his hand! That
very morning he had put an end to his
wretched being. A paper was found upon
the table, of his own hand writing, which
imported that he had entirely ruined himfelf and a moft amiable wife and child,
and that life was infupportable to him.

RIVALSHIP WITHOUT ENMITY;
EMULATION WITHOUT ENVY.

DEMOSTHENES, a celebrated Gre-
cian Orator, was born at Athens,
near four hundred years before the Chriftian
Era. He was remarkable for the fimplicity and energy of his eloquence. It is
faid that he copied the Hiftory of Thucy-
dides no lefs than eight times, to acquire a
nervous

nervous and majeftic diction; and that his thirft after knowledge was fo great, as to lead him to purfue his ftudies in a fubterranean apartment, that he might be free from noife, difturbance, or interruption.

Æschines was alfo an eminent Orator of Greece, and cotemporary with Demofthenes. He preferred an indictment againft Ctefiphon, as a pretext for the accufation of his rival Demofthenes. A day was appointed for the trial, and no caufe ever excited fuch general curiofity, or was conducted with greater pomp and folemnity. People affembled from every part of Greece, to be fpectators of the conteft between thefe two great mafters of rhetoric. The inclinations of the Citizens were favourable to Æfchines; but fuch was the prevailing eloquence of his antagonift, that he loft his caufe, and was fentenced to banifhment. He retired to the ifland of Rhodes; where he eftablifhed a School of Oratory, which continued to flourifh many centuries afterwards. He commenced his Lectures with the Oration which he had delivered

juft

juft before his exile; and it was highly ap-
plauded by the audience. But when he recited the anfwer of Demofthenes, his hear-
ers redoubled their expreffions of admiration. Æfchines, fo far from feeling any
emotions of envy at this fecond triumph of
his rival, cried out with rapture, *How
great, my friends, would have been your
tranfport, had you heard Demofthenes himfelf deliver this oration, with thofe invincible
powers of elocution for which he is fo juftly
and univerfally celebrated?*

WHEN Æfchines was condemned to banifhment, Demofthenes exulted not in the
victory which he had obtained; but followed his rival to the fhip in which he was
to embark, and conftrained him to accept
of a fum of money, to defray the expences
of his voyage, and to procure for him an
eafy fettlement at Rhodes. Impreffed with
this affecting inftance of generofity, the
exiled Orator with admiration exclaimed,
*How deeply muft I regret the lofs of a country,
in which I have received fuch liberal affiftance
from a profeffed enemy, as I cannot expect*
M 4   *even*

even from a friend in any other part of the world !

CICERO.

————

VIRTUOUS FRIENDSHIP EXTENDS BEYOND
THE GRAVE.

EMILIA had been flightly indifpofed
feveral days; but not in fuch a manner as to confine her from the chearful
fociety of her brothers and fifters. Whilft
fhe was ftanding in the midft of them, a
fainting fit fuddenly overpowered her, and
fhe fell down as it were lifelefs on the floor.
She was foon recovered by the tender offices of Sophronia; but the affecting image
of death, which the children had feen,
continued for fome time to imprefs their
minds with forrow and terror. Alexis, in
the evening, accompanied his father into
the fields. The path which they purfued
led them to the banks of the Irwell; where
they ftopped to contemplate its winding
ftream and checquered fides. The ftump
of a tree, overfhadowed by a neighbouring
oak,

oak, afforded them a comfortable feat; and Euphronius began to expatiate on the wifdom and goodnefs of Providence, in watering the earth with rivers, which flow into the fea, and are again returned in fertilifing fhowers. Alexis made no reply; and Euphronius obferving that he was loft in thought, inquired what fubject fo deeply engaged his attention. The youth faid with a figh, I have been early taught to fee, admire, and reverence the Deity in all his works; but more particularly in the ftructure of man; in his prefent enjoyments, and future expectations. The moral affections you have cultivated in my heart with affiduous care; and I have fondly believed that the exercife of them will conftitute my chief felicity through all eternity. Oh! that the pleafing delufion had been ftill continued! This morning I was fhocked with the apparent death of my beloved Emilia; but it was fome confolation to my mind, that we fhould hereafter meet again; renew our fond regard; and for ever live together in the fame endearing connection which now fubfifts between

us.

us. In this hope, it feems, I was miferably miftaken. A learned Divine, whofe works I have juft been reading, afferts with confidence, that in Heaven, the virtuous of all ages, paft, prefent, and to come, will dwell together, as in one univerfal family, without perfonal partialities or diftinction.

THE doctrine, I truft, is falfe, replied Euphronius, with fome emotion; for Heaven, me thinks, would not be fo to me if it were true. But I correct myfelf, Alexis: On a fubject of fuch uncertainty, we fhould fpeak with an awful reliance on that great Being, who perfectly knows our frame, and what will beft promote our happinefs. With fuch fentiments of reverence let us purfue the interefting theme; and inquire whether reafon and revelation do not juftify the hope, that we fhall hereafter be united to our virtuous relations and friends; and enjoy, with increafing delight, all thofe tender attachments, which, in the prefent ftate, fweeten both focial and domeftic life.

ONE

ONE of the ftrongeft arguments for the future exiftence of the foul, derived from the light of nature, is the dread which we feel of annihilation, and our ardent defires after immortality. Have we not the like anxiety, again to be reftored, in happier regions, to thofe whom, in this world, we have known, efteemed, and loved ? The human underftanding feems to be formed for *endlefs* improvement. The faculty of *comprehenfion* is daily enlarged, till the animal machine, having acquired its full vigour, fuffers the gradual decays of age : And as the Deity hath created nothing in vain, *capacity* may be fuppofed to imply *attainment*, in fome other ftage of our exiftence.

BUT fhall we grant to our *intellectual*, a privilege which we deny to our *moral* powers; or exclude from future growth and cultivation, the nobleft and moft important endowments of the mind? The principle of benevolence is neither inconfiftent with the partialities of friendfhip, nor with the endearments of family love; but rather
                                                    ther

ther originates from them, like circles on
the water, widening as they flow from one
common centre. Nor will the filial, parental, or fraternal charities damp the fer-
vour of our piety to the FATHER of the
Univerfe ; or abate our gratitude to the
great Bond of our union, and the Author
of our deareft enjoyments. The prefent
life is only the commencement of thofe improvements in knowledge and goodnefs,
which we fhall progreffively make through
all eternity. And as our kindred and
friends are, in a peculiar manner, the companions of our journey here, and the objects of our moft virtuous affections; is it not
probable that they will continue to be fuch
hereafter; and that we fhall not only find
them our *crown of rejoicing*, but that it will
be our divineft pleafure to promote the advancement of each other in piety, glory,
and felicity ? The Scriptures fpeak not ex-
plicitly concerning this interefting point;
but there are a variety of paffages in the
New Teftament, which evidently imply
that good men " will be happy hereafter
" in the fame feats of joy ; will live under
                                    " the

" the fame perfect government; and be
" members of the fame heavenly fociety.
" Will not then our neareft relations be ac-
" ceffible to us ? and if acceffible, fhall we
" not fly to them, and mingle our hearts and
" fouls again ? "

" THE Theffalonians, a little before St.
" Paul wrote his firft Epiftle to them, had
" loft fome of their friends by death. In
" thefe circumftances, he exhorts them not
" to *forrow like others who had no hope*;
" becaufe they might conclude certainly
" from the death and refurrection of Jefus,
" that thofe who *had flept in him, God*
" *would hereafter bring with him.* He tells
" them *by the word of the Lord*, or as from
" immediate revelation, that a period was
" coming, when Chrift would defcend
" from Heaven *with a fhout ; with the*
" *voice of the Arch-angel, and with the trump*
" *of God;* and when the friends they had
" loft fhould be raifed from the dead, and
" together with themfelves, *fhould be caught*
" *up to meet the Lord in the air, and to live*
" *for ever with him.* But what I have in
" view

" view is more diftinctly aflerted in the fe-
" cond Chapter of this Epiftle, Ver. 19.
" *For what is our hope, our joy, our crown*
" *of rejoicing? Are not even ye in the pre-*
" *fence of our Lord Jefus at his coming?* It
" is moft plainly implied in thefe words,
" that the Apoftle expected to fee and
" know again his Theffalonian converts,
" at Chrift's fecond coming. The fame
" remark may be made on his words in
" the Corinthians. *Knowing that he, who*
" *raifed up the Lord Jefus, fhall raife us up*
" *alfo by Jefus, and prefent us with you. As*
" *you have acknowledged us in part, that we*
" *are your rejoicing, even fo ye alfo are ours*
" *in the day of the Lord Jefus.*" *(x)*

THUS it appears that the pleafing idea
of a re-union with our virtuous relations
and friends, in the future life, is agreeable
to the natural expectations of mankind;
neceffary to the exercife of our moft diftinguifhed moral powers; and favourable to
every fentiment of gratitude, devotion,
and

(x) See Dr. Price's Differtations on Providence, Prayer. &c.
P. 233.

and piety. Revelation feems alfo to confirm what reafon fo much approves ; and I
hope, my dear Alexis, your mind is now
no longer difquieted with defpondency or
fear. Indulge the generous affections of
your heart ; cherifh the filial and fraternal
love with which it glows ; cultivate the
valuable friendfhips you have formed ; and
be affured that what conftitues your prefent,
will heighten your future felicity. But remember that your union in the heavenly
world, can only be with the worthy and
the good ; and be cautious to form no o-
ther clofe attachments, but fuch as will
merit perpetuity. If Death fnatch from
you a beloved friend, whilft you lament the
lofs, *forrow not as one without hope* or confolation. The feparation, however painful,
will be but for a feafon ; and you will have
a kindred fpirit in the regions of blifs, to
welcome your arrival there, and to conduct
you into the glorious prefence of the Sove-
reign of the Univerfe.

O! præclarum diem, fays Cicero, *cum ad*
illud divinum animorum concilium cœtumque
proficifcar

proficiscar; cumque ex hac turba, et colluvi-
one discedam! proficiscar enim ad Catonem
meum, quo nemo vir melior natus est, nemo
pietate præstantior!   Cic. de Senectute.

WARMTH in ARGUMENT.

LORD Shaftesbury, I remember, in his
excellent Characteristics, relates the
story of a Clown, who was present at the
debates of the Doctors in the University
of Oxford. Though he was equally a
stranger to the subjects and the language,
he seemed to listen with great attention,
and to receive much pleasure from them.
A Gentleman Commoner who stood near
him, and observed the emotions expressed
in his countenance, inquired what amusement he could find in hearing such dif-
putes, since it was impossible that he
should even know to which side the victory
inclined. *Sir*, replied the Clown, *I am
not such a fool as you imagine me to be; for
I can easily see who is first put into a passion.*
Common sense dictated this observation to
the

the Country Man, that he who was superior
in argument would maintain his compo-
sure of mind; whilst his antagonist would
naturally become violent and angry, because unable to support his cause by the
force of reason.

HABITS of SENSUALITY may be formed
in early YOUTH.

FLORIO and Alonzo were schoolfellows,
and inseparable companions at Eton.
They were both profusely supplied with
money by their too indulgent parents; and
they spent it, not in the pursuit of active
diversions, in the purchase of books, or in
the offices of humanity, but in cakes, tarts,
and sweet-meats. With these they con-
tinually glutted themselves; and as the
head is always stupified when the stomach
is overloaded; they were the greatest
dunces in the school. Florio, whose powers
of digestion were much feebler than those
of his friend, became pale and emaciated
as he grew in stature. His appetite was
nice and delicate, and he loathed every

N   kind

kind of food, but fuch as afforded the moft
favoury and exquifite relifh. I have feen
him rife from a good dinner without eating
a fingle morfel, becaufe the meat was
plainly dreffed, and the fauces had no
poignancy. Thus he often ftarved in the
midft of plenty; and loft the only enjoyment, which life was capable- of affording
to his vitiated tafte. His fortune was foon
expended in the gratification of his palate;
and he was reduced to practife the meaneft
arts, to obtain fupplies for frefh indul-
gences. He has been known to purchafe an
Ortolan with the guinea which he begged
as charity; and to give for a difh of green
peafe, a much larger fum with which he
was entrufted, for the relief of a friend in
diftrefs *(y)*.

ALONZO, whofe ftrength of conftitution
converted into nourifhment the unwhole-
fome paftry which he fo greedily devoured,
became lufty, and corpulent; but his complexion was wan, his flefh bloated, and
his

(y) This fact is related of the late Theophilus Cibber.

his belly unnaturally fwoln. His appetite was rather voracious than nice; and he confumed as much food at one meal, as would have fufficed, with temperance, for three. He died of an apoplexy at the age of thirty; having gorged himfelf with fuch quantities of meat, at a public entertainment, as occafioned a fudden ceffation of the animal and vital functions.

SENSUALITY is a vice which contaminates the body, depreffes the underftanding, deadens the moral feelings of the heart, and degrades the human fpecies from the exalted rank which they hold in the creation (z). It is fhocking to read the examples of it, which both antient and modern hiftory afford. And as the Spartans ufed to make their flaves drunk, to difplay to their children the folly and odioufnefs of intemperance; I fhall recite a few in-

N 2 ftances

(z) --------- Vides ut pallidus omnis
Coenâ defurgat dubiâ? quin corpus onuftum
Hefternis Vitijs animum quoque prægravat unâ,
Atque affigit humo divinæ particulam auræ.

Hor. Sat 2. Lib. 2. Ver. 76.

ſtances of extravagance in eating, as the beſt leſſons of moderation and abſtinence.

Lucullus, a Roman General, kept the moſt magnificent table; and was ſerved in the ſame ſumptuous manner, even when no gueſts were invited. His Steward, one day, made an apology for the dinner, which was leſs ſplendid than uſual; and hoped it would be excuſed, as there was no company. "Did you not know," ſaid the Epicure, "that Lucullus was to eat "with Lucullus to-day?" Cicero and Pompey had heard much of his mode of living; and they were determined to ſurpriſe him, by going, without notice, to partake of his entertainment. He ordered the dinner to be ſerved in the Hall of Apollo; and it was prepared in ſo ſhort a time, and with ſo much opulence, as aſtoniſhed his viſitors. The Hall of Apollo was a private direction, underſtood by the cooks to imply, that the feaſt ſhould amount to near twelve hundred pounds ſterling *(a)*.

MARK

(a) Plut. in Lucullo. ----- Dr. Arbuthnot eſtimates the expence at £1614 : 11 : 8.

MARK ANTHONY paffed his time in re-
vels and entertainments, whilft he was with
Cleopatra in Egypt. A young Greek,
then profecuting the ftudy of Phyfic at
Alexandria, had the curiofity to go into
his kitchen, where he faw eight wild boars
roafting, at the fame time, before the fire.
He inquired what number of guefts were
to be at fupper. Not more than ten, faid
an Officer fmiling; but it is neceffary that
every part of the animal fhould be brought
to the table in exquifite perfection (b).

CLODIUS ÆSOPUS, the moft famous
Tragedian that ever appeared on the Roman
ftage, and who acquired a princely fortune
by his profeffion as an actor, had one difh
which coft fix thoufand feftertia, that is
four thoufand eight hundred pounds fter-
ling(c). It confifted of the choiceft and
deareft finging birds, brought perhaps
from the moft diftant provinces of the
Empire.

N 3 THE

<hr>

(b) Id.
(c) See Plin. l. 10. c. 60. Arbuthnot on Coins p. 133.

The name of Sir Ifaac Newton is not at
this time more famous amongſt Philoſo-
phers, than that of Apicius was formerly
with the Roman Epicures. The Capital
of the World had the honour of giving
birth, at different periods of time, to three
of this denomination; who were all celebrated for their gluttony. The one, who
was moſt eminent, lived under the reigns
of Auguſtus and Tiberius, and read public
Lectures on the art of Senſuality. He
was the inventor of a cake which was called by his name; and he wrote an elaborate
Treatiſe on the methods of ſtimulating the
appetite, *de Gulæ irritamentis*. Hiſtorians
of credit aſſert, that he ſailed from *Min-
turnæ* in *Campania* to Africa, with no other
view than to taſte of a ſpecies of oyſters,
reported to be much larger and more delicious than any on the coaſt of Italy;
but finding that he had received falſe information, he returned immediately without condeſcending, and probably without
feeling the leaſt curioſity to go on ſhore.
After ſquandering immenſe ſums of money
in

in the moſt ſhameful luxury, *(d)* he poiſon-
ed himſelf, from an apprehenſion of being
ſtarved, though he had a very ample fortune remaining.

THE Emperor Heliogabalus, that mon-
ſter of cruelty and beſtiality, is ſaid to have
had the brains of ſeveral hundred Oſtriches
dreſſed for one diſh. *(e)* But it is painful to

N 4　　　　　relate

(d) £807. 291 : 13 : 4. according to Dr. Arbuthnot's
calculation.

(e) Senſuality ſeems to be a weed which ſprings up in every ſoil; and has been diſcovered where opulence and the arts
of luxury are little known, and where we ſhould expect to
meet only with the ſimplicity of nature. The following paſſage from Mr. Forſter's Voyage to the South Seas, will evince
the truth of this obſervation, and exhibit a new mode of Epi-
curiſm.

" OUR walk continued along the ſhore (of Otaheite) be-
" yond another marai, much like the firſt, to a neat houſe,
" where a very fat man, who ſeemed to be a chief of the diſ-
" trict, was lolling on his wooden pillow. Before him two
" ſervants were preparing his deſert, by beating up with water
" ſome bread fruit and bananas, in a large wooden bowl, and
" mixing with it a quantity of the fermented ſour paſte of
" bread fruit called mahei. The conſiſtence of this mixture
" was ſuch, that it could not properly be called a drink, and
" the inſtrument with which they made it was a peſtle of a
" black

relate fuch inftances of depravity. The mind fickens at the contemplation of rational and immortal beings, funk fo low in the fcale of animated nature. And it feems almoft neceffary to vindicate the honour of our fpecies, by placing in contraft a few oppofite examples.

TIMOTHEUS, an Athenian Commander, of the moft diftinguifhed reputation, was invited to fup with Plato. The Philofopher entertained him with a decent, but frugal repaft; feafoned however with fuch chearful and inftructive converfation, as made the General highly delighted with his reception. When he met Plato the fucceeding day in the city, he accofted him in a moft friendly manner, and thanked him

---

" black polifhed ftone, which appeared to be a kind of Bifal-
" tes. While this was doing, a woman who fat near him,
" crammed down his throat by handfuls the remains of a large
" baked fifh, and feveral bread fruits which he fwallowed with
" a voracious appetite. His countenance was the picture of
" phlegmatic infenfibility, and feemed to witnefs that all his
" thoughts centered in the care of his paunch. He fcarce
" deigned to look at us, and a few monofyllables which he ut-
" tered were only directed to remind his feeders of their duty,
" when we attracted their attention."

him for the very agreeable feaft which he had enjoyed. " For your entertainment," faid he, " was not only grateful whilft it " lafted, but has left a relifh which conti- " nues to this moment." *(f)*

Socrates ufed to fay, that he *eat to live*, and left to others the fenfual fatisfaction of *living only to eat*. Having invited a company of Gentlemen to fupper, his wife Xantippe was afhamed of the humble fare provided for them. " Be not anxious on " that account," faid Socrates; " for if " my vifitors be men of temperance and " underftanding, they will be well fatisfi- " ed; and if they be of an oppofite cha- " racter, they deferve no indulgence." *(g)*

When Agefilaus, King of Sparta, was prefented by the Thafians with a large quantity of the moft delicious eatables, and coftly liquors, he directed the whole to be diftributed amongft the flaves, who ferved
in

(f) Cicero.
(g) Plutarch.

in the camp. The Thaſians, with the utmoſt ſurpriſe, demanded the reaſon of his
conduct; and he nobly replied, *It is be-*
neath the character of men of probity and
courage to provoke and corrupt their appetites
with dainties. Such delicacies are fit only for
ſlaves, who aſpire to no higher pleaſures than
thoſe of eating and drinking; and to them I
have therefore diſpoſed of your preſents (h).

ALEXANDER, in the prime of life and in
the midſt of victories, behaved on a ſimilar
occaſion with equal wiſdom and magnanimity. For when Ada, Queen of Caria, ſent
him meats dreſſed in the moſt exquiſite
manner, and ſkilful cooks of every kind;
he informed her that theſe favours were of
little value to him, ſince his governor,
Leonidas, had long ſince furniſhed him
with two of the beſt miniſters to his appetite, temperance and exerciſe.

I ſhall conclude this article with the
following paſſage from Petrarch, a celebrated

(h) Ibid.

brated Italian Poet, whofe fociety was courted by men of the higheft rank, and who,
notwithftanding he had free accefs to the
luxurious tables of Bifhops, Cardinals,
Princes and Popes, thus expreffes himfelf
concerning the *pleafures* of *eating.* " I
" prefer the moft fimple meats, prepared
" without art or labour; and think that no
" cheer is more delicious than the fruits
" and herbs of my garden. I always ap-
" proved a tafte conformable to nature.
" Not that I diflike a good repaft now and
" then; but it fhould come very rarely.
" Among the Romans, before the Conqueft
" of Afia, the cook was the vileft of flaves:
" Would to God! they had never conquer-
" ed that part of the world, which fubdued
" them by its foftnefs and luxury."

The GLUTTON.

THE Glutton is an animal of the
Weefel kind, and is fo called from
his voracious appetite. He is found in the
northern parts of Europe, Afia, and America,

rica, and is ufually about three feet long, and a foot and a half high. His body is long, his legs fhort, and he takes his prey by furprife, and not by purfuit. He climbs a tree, and lurks amongft the thick branches of it, until a Deer or fome other large animal paffes underneath, upon whofe back he impetuoufly cafts himfelf; and remaining there firm and unfhaken, by the ftrength and fharpnefs of his claws, he eats the neck, and digs a paffage to the great blood veffels which lie in that part. The affrighted and agonifing Deer flies in vain. His infatiable foe continues to feaft upon him; and when he drops, leaves him not till he has confumed the whole carcafe. When the ftomach of the Glutton has been thus gorged, he lies torpid feveral days, then awakes again to afcend fome neighbouring tree, in queft of another adventure.

The fkin of this animal is covered with a fur, which is highly valued for its beauty and luftre.

The ASS.

THE Duke of Bridgewater's **Canal** terminates about a quarter of a mile from Manchefter. One branch of it communicates with Leverpool, by the river Merfey, into which it falls below Runcorn; another is carried into the center of his Grace's Collieries at Worfeley, and by means of it this town and neighbourhood are fupplied with large quantities of **coal**. Small loads are permitted to be fold, for the benefit of the poor; and a confiderable number of little carts, each drawn by a fingle afs, are conftantly employed to convey and diftribute this article, fo neceffary to the comfort, and even to the fupport of life.

ONE frofty day, about noon, Euphronius walked towards the Duke's Wharf, accompanied by Alexis and Jacobus. As they were defcending a flope in the road, which the ice had rendered almoft as flip-

pery

pery as glaſs, they turned on one ſide to make way for an Aſs, with a cart very heavily laden. The little animal exerted all his powers, and ſtrained every nerve to aſcend the brow: But all his efforts were in vain; his feet ſlided; he fell upon his knees; and the cart rolled down the declivity, dragging backwards the affrighted Aſs. Provoked at this diſappointment, the driver laſhed the poor beaſt in the moſt unmerciful manner; yet could not, by his utmoſt ſeverity, urge him to a ſecond attempt. He remained invincible and immoveable; and as if equally conſcious of his inability and of his ſervitude, he bore with patient but inert ſubmiſſion, the cruel ſtripes that were inflicted on him.

Euphronius interpoſed in favour of the Aſs; but neither reaſon, entreaty, nor menaces availed; and the carter continued his blows till Jacobus offered the few halfpence which he had in his poſſeſſion, to bribe him to humanity. The little party now proceeded in their walk, and were highly entertained with the various materials

materials for the manufactures of Manchefter, which lay piled in heaps around them.
Their refpective ufes were confidered, and
the diverfified exertions of human art and
induftry afforded the moft copious and
pleafing topics of converfation. Whilft
they were thus engaged, a loud huzza
was heard, and the curiofity of Alexis in-
duced him to pafs onwards to a number
of men, from whom it proceeded, and
who were ftanding together in a circle on
the Wharf. Juft as he approached them,
another fhout of joy was raifed; and he
learned, that each individual prefent was
deciding, by the throw of a halfpenny,
whether the Mule, or Afs, employed in
his cart, fhould have a feed of corn at noon,
or whether the value of the provender
fhould be applied to the purchafe of fpiri-
tuous liquors for himfelf: And whenever
chance proved favourable to injuftice and
debauchery, the whole crowd united in the
cry of exultation. Euphronius, fhocked
with this account, retired from the Wharf,
deeming it vain to expoftulate with men,
who appeared to be devoid of all humanity,

ty, and who would have filenced his remonftrances by rudenefs and abufe.   But
to his fons, as they walked along, he
explained and enforced the indifpenfable
obligation we are under, to provide fufficient fupplies of food for every creature,
that is dependent on us.   And he quoted
the divine command, *Thou fhalt not muzzle
the ox, when he treadeth out the corn*, as
extending to all the animals, which are
fubfervient to our benefit.   Intereft indeed,
with refpect to many of them, hath conftrained us to pay fome attention to this
duty : But the poor Afs feems to be regarded, as an outcaft of nature; and after
a day of toil and drudgery, he is turned
into the lanes, during the hours which
fhould be devoted to fleep, to collect a
fcanty and precarious meal, which ferves
rather to excite, than to fatisfy the cravings
of his appetite.   His tamenefs, humility,
and patience, inftead of raifing pity and
regard, have expofed him to contempt, to
infult, and oppreffion.   We defpife his
fervices, becaufe they are purchafed cheap-
ly ; we overload him with our burdens,
                                                because

becaufe he is paffive under them ; we fcourge him with capricious feverity, becaufe he fubmits to the rod; and we deny him proper fuftenance, becaufe he is tolerant of hunger, and contented with the weeds, which other animals reject. Yet is the Afs, in that ftate of freedom for which nature formed him, active, fierce and impetuous. In the defarts of Lybia and Numidia, and in fome parts of South America, when purfued by the hunter, he runs with amazing fwiftnefs ; and neither declivities nor precipices can ftop his career. If attacked, he defends himfelf with courage and intrepidity : But the moment he is overpowered, his fpirit becomes depreffed ; his ferocity deferts him; and he foon contracts the dulnefs and ftupidity, which characterife his fpecies, in all thofe countries, where he is reduced to fervitude.

THE Perfians efteem his flefh a very delicate repaft ; but a warm climate feems to be neceffary to its tendernefs and flavour. In proportion to his bulk, the Afs is ftronger than the Horfe ; he is alfo more
healthy,

healthy, and lefs liable to ftart, or ftumble. He is fond of his mafter, although fo often abufed by him; fcents him at a diftance, and diftinguifhes him from others in a crowd. His eyes are remarkably good, · and his fenfe of hearing is acute. The nicety of this animal is worthy of notice. He drinks only of the cleareft ftreams, and without putting his nofe into the water; fears to wet his feet; and turns out of the way to avoid the miry parts of a road. The period of his life extends from twenty to thirty years. Mr. Buffon fays, that the She-Afs exceeds the Male in longevity; which he afcribes to the relaxation of her flavery, during the feafons of pregnancy. But the fame obfervation has been made of the Hare, which lives in a ftate of nature; and it may perhaps hold true of a variety of other animals. In the Human Species it has been fully evinced, that the life of Males is much more frail, than that of

---

(i) See Dr. Price's Treatife on Reverfionary Payments; and the Author's Obfervations on the State of Population in Manchefter, and other adjacent Places; Effays philofophical, medical, and experimental.

of Females, even in the earlieſt ſtages of it, antecedent to all hardſhip or excefs(i).

THE ſkin of the Aſs is firm and elaſtic. Sieves, drums, ſhoes, and a ſort of parchment for pocket books are made of it. The Orientals alſo manufacture it into what we call ſhagreen. It is probable, that the bones of this animal, like the hide, are of a very ſolid and compact texture. The Ancients formed them into flutes; and they are ſaid to have been peculiarly ſonorous. Aſſes' milk differs eſſentially from that of the Cow. It is neither diſpoſed to turn four, nor is it capable of being reduced to a curd; though, by ſtanding, it depoſites a mucilaginous part, and affords a conſiderable quantity of whey. Very little cream is obtained from it; and this cream is not convertible into butter. If the whey be evaporated, it yields a much larger proportion of ſaline and ſaccharine matter, than the milk of any other animal. From theſe qualities are derived the well-known medicinal powers of Aſſes milk.

PRIDE

PRIDE and PEDANTRY.

JULIUS returned from Cambridge, elated with certain academical honours, which had been conferred upon him. He had anticipated, in his imagination, the joy with which he fhould infpire his parents; the congratulations of his friends; and the refpect and deference, which would be fhewn him by all his former companions. Full of fuch ideal importance, he received the compliments of thofe who came to vifit him, with haughty civility, and mortifying condefcenfion. Inftead of obliging inquiries concerning their families or connections, he talked to them only of himfelf, or of his College acquaintance; and eagerly feized every opportunity of difplaying the fuperiority of his knowledge, and the eftimation in which he was held by his Profeffors, and by Fellow Commoners of the higheft rank. His vanity and oftentation foon excited univerfal difguft; and his pertnefs and paffion for difputing involved him in numberlefs quarrels. What-

ever

ever opinion was advanced, he immediately controverted it; and by puzzling his
antagonift with definitions and logical diftinctions, he feldom failed to obtain a victory, and to create an enemy. He had
unfortunately adopted that fyftem of fcep-
tical philofophy, which denies exiftence to
Matter; and he ftrenuoufly maintained,
that all external objects are only things
perceived by fenfe: And what do we perceive, faid he, but our own ideas and fenfations? What are light and colours, heat
and cold, extenfion and figure, but fo
many fenfations, ideas, or mental impreffions? It is impoffible, even in thought,
to feparate thefe from perception; and no
truth can be more felf evident, than that
all the forms of body, both in heaven
above and on the earth beneath, are mere
phantafms, and have their exiftence in the
mind alone *(k)*. By the frequent and unfeafonable introduction of thefe opinions,
fo contradictory to the common fenfe and
conviction of mankind, he damped the

O 3   pleafures

(k) See Bifhop Berkely and Mr. Hume.

pleafures of focial intercourfe, and became burthenfome to the whole circle of his father's friends. It happened, in the month of January, that he was invited to dine, with many other Gentlemen, at the houfe of Sempronius, who refided in the country. The day was intenfely cold, and the ground was covered with fnow. Julius, as he rode along, foon entered upon his favourite topic, with the companions of his vifit; and ridiculed them for fhivering at what he had proved to be only a conceit of their own minds. Whilft he was laughing at their folly, his horfe plunged into a deep drift, and overwhelmed himfelf and his rider with fnow. Julius, terrified with the accident, called aloud for affiftance; but his fellow travellers were for fome time deaf to his entreaties. They retorted his jokes, and would not attempt to extricate him, till he was ftarved into a confeffion, of the *reality of cold*. The fnow had penetrated his cloaths, and his boots were filled with water: He therefore haftened forward to the houfe of Sempronius, where having changed his garments, and being feated at the

the table near a glowing fire, he foon banifhed all recollection of his late misfortune. The entertainment was plentiful and elegant, and the guefts found their appetites fharpened by the weather, and by the ride which they had taken. Julius was exceedingly hungry, and was beginning to fall voracioufly upon a flice of beef, to which he had been helped, when his fervant called off his attention, by a meffage that he delivered to him. His face being turned afide from the table, the Gentleman on his right hand conveyed away the piece of beef, and appropriated it to his own ufe. Julius now refumed, with eagernefs, his knife and fork, but finding his plate empty, he complained, in very bitter terms, of the depredation which had been committed. The feaft was fufpended; and all that were prefent rejoiced in the difappointment of Julius. They urged to him, that eating *was an ideal pleafure, and that fpirit can require no fuftenance.* Sempronius, however, politely reftrained the general mirth on this occafion, becaufe it was enjoyed at the expence of an individual, who had a claim

O 4 to

to his good offices and protection; and he sent him a fresh supply of beef. When the cravings of nature were satisfied, Julius began to feel that he was seated too near the fire: He durst not, however, express his uneasiness, lest he should draw upon himself some new mortification. But the heat at length became intolerable, and he started up from his seat, exclaiming that he should be burnt to death. Vain, however, was the attempt to change his situation. The chair, in which he had been sitting, was closely wedged by the two contiguous ones; and he stood a laughing stock for the whole company. *Fire has no warmth in it*, said one to him: Look through the windows, said another, and the snow which you behold on the distant hills, will *cool* your *perception* of *heat*, by the contrary *perception* of *cold*. Julius could no longer endure the raillery, which was poured upon him. He forcibly pushed back his chair, and took his leave of the company, by assuring them, that for the future it should be his maxim to *think with the wise, and talk with the vulgar*.

JULIUS

JULIUS had acquired great credit at Cambridge by his compofitions. They were elegant, animated, and judicious; and feveral prizes, at different times, had been adjudged to him. An Oration, which he delivered the week before he left the Univerfity, had been honoured with particular applaufe; and on his return home, he was impatient to gratify his vanity, and to extend his reputation, by having it read to a number of his father's literary friends. A party was therefore collected; and after dinner the manufcript was produced. Julius declined the office of reader, becaufe he had contracted a hoarfenefs on his journey; and a conceited young man, with great forwardnefs, offered his fervices. Whilft he was fettling himfelf on his feat, licking his lips, adjufting his mouth, hawking, hemming, and making other ridiculous preparations for the performance, which he had undertaken, a profound filence reigned through the company, the united effect of attention and expectation. Alexis, whom Euphronius had carried with him to this entertainment,

tainment, employed the prefent interval in
watching the countenance of Julius; and
he fympathifed in the anxiety, which he
faw expreffed in every feature of his face.
The reader at length began; but his tone
of voice was fo fhrill and diffonant, his utterance fo vehement, his pronunciation fo
affected, his emphafis fo injudicious, and
his accents were fo improperly placed, that
good manners alone reftrained the laughter
of the audience. Julius was all this while
upon the rack, and his arm was more than
once extended, to fnatch his compofition
from the coxcomb who delivered it. But
he proceeded, with full confidence in his
own elocution, uniformly overftepping, as
Shakefpear expreffes it, the modefty of
nature.

> With ftudied improprieties of fpeech,
> He foars beyond the hackney critic's reach;
> To *epithets* allots emphatic ftate,
> Whilft *principals* ungraced, like lacquies wait.
> Conjunction, prepofition, adverb join
> To ftamp new vigour on the nervous line.
> In monofyllables his thunders roll,
> HE, SHE, IT, AND, WE, YE, THEY, fright the foul.
>   CHURCHILL.

WHEN

WHEN the Oration was concluded, the
Gentlemen returned their thanks to the
Author; but the compliments which they
paid him, were more expreffive of politenefs and civility, than of a conviction of
his merit. Indeed the beauties of his compofition had been converted, by bad reading, into blemifhes, and the fenfe of it
rendered obfcure and even unintelligible.
Julius and his father could not conceal
their vexation and difappointment; and
the guefts, perceiving that they laid them
under a painful reftraint, withdrew as foon
as decency permitted, to their refpective
habitations.

THE Poet has obferved, that

" Of all the conquefts which vain mortals boaft,
By wit, by valour, or by wifdom won,
The firft and faireft in a young man's eye
Is woman's captive heart."

JULIUS panted for fuch a victory; he
believed himfelf to be the object of the
ladies *admiration*; but was ambitious to be
diftinguifhed by their *love*. And he offered

ed his ardent vows at the fhrine of every
fair damfel, with whom he converfed.
Daphne, however, was the haughty mai-
den, whom he wifhed moft to fubdue.
Againft her heart he directed all the amo-
rous artillery of ancient lore; and he woo-
ed her, not as a Venus or Minerva, but as
a divinity, who united in her fingle perfon,
the graces and attributes of each nymph
and goddefs, in the heathen mythology.
But as the ideas of beauty are varied by
time, caprice, and fafhion, his claffical
compliments were not always acceptable.
Thus when he afcribed to her the coldnefs
of Vefta, and the chaftity of Diana, fhe
hung down her head in bafhful confufion:
but when in the poetical language of Homer,
Horace, Ovid, and Tibullus, he praifed her
oxen eyes, bufhy eyebrows, golden treffes, and
plump bofom, fhe received with difdain the
incenfe of flattery, which was formerly fo
grateful to the ladies of antiquity. For fhe
had taken infinite pains to pluck her eyebrows, to change from red to auburne the
colour of her hair, and to contract her
bulk by the trammels of whalebone.   Julius

lius in reality was not the favourite of
Daphne. Modefty, gentlenefs, and fimplicity of manners were charms that he
wanted, to render him agreeable; and her
heart had been long in the poffeffion of a
youth, who undervalued a prize which he
had too eafily obtained. To fix her roving
lover, by alarming his fears and roufing his
jealoufy, fhe liftened, with apparent approbation, to the addreffes of Julius; and his
boafting foon enfured the fuccefs of her
ftratagem. As he was haftening to her
houfe one morning, with an ode to beauty,
which he had juft written in imitation of
Anacreon, he faw her at a diftance, paffing
out of a private door of the church, habit-
ed in white, and accompanied by his rival,
in the drefs of a bridegroom. As one
thunder-ftruck, he ftood appalled and
motionlefs, till recovered to his fenfes
by the delivery of the following billet:
"Daphne, perfuaded that Julius courted
himfelf and not her, leaves him in the full
enjoyment of his miftrefs, who will remain
with conftancy the dear object of his vanity, admiration, and love."

SUCH

Such were the varied mortifications which Julius fuffered. By degrees, however, they produced the moft falutary effects upon his mind ; correcting his arrogance, humbling his pride, and teaching him the art of felf government. Experience convinced him, that learning is only refpected, when it is rather concealed, than oftentatioufly difplayed ; that fuperiority, when affumed, is feldom admitted, and generally rejected with fcorn ; and that to make others pleafed with us, we muft endeavour, by attention and proper deference, to render them fatisfied and pleafed with themfelves.

VANITY.

CICERO left Sicily, where he had been Quæftor, full of the flattering idea, that he was the fubject of general converfation in Italy, and that he fhould every where be honoured with marks of the higheft diftinction, for the wifdom and integrity which he had difplayed in that

arduous

arduous office. He happened to pafs through Puzzoli in the feafon when crowds of company reforted to the celebrated baths of that place. " Pray what news, faid one to him ? Is it long fince you came from Rome ? I am returning from my province, replied Cicero, with great furprife. True, obferved another, from Africa! No, anfwered Cicero, with indignation, from Sicily. You furely know, interpofed a third, that he has been Quæftor at Syracufe." This was a farther inftance of mortifying ignorance, for his province lay in a different part of the ifland : and Cicero, abafhed and difgufted, turned away from the company, to avoid any more interrogations. Reflection, however, he informs us, converted this difappointment into a leffon of inftruction, and he derived advantages from it, which overbalanced the lofs of compliment and admiration *(1)*.

KNOW-

(1) Vid. Cic. Orat. pro Planc,

K N O W L E D G E.

ABOUT ten years fince, Mr. Charles
Miller of the botanic garden at Cambridge, raifed from a fingle grain of wheat,
in a fpace of time not much exceeding
twelve months, three pecks and three quar-
ters of corn, or about five hundred and
feventy-fix thoufand eight hundred and
forty grains. An aftonifhing multiplication! produced by repeatedly dividing the
ftems, feparating the fide fhoots, and
tranfplanting both.

NOT lefs capable of increafe is every
feed of knowledge, if fown in a fertile underftanding, and cultivated with the fame
affiduity, fkill and perfeverance. Demon-
ftrate to the human mind the exiftence of
God, and from this root all the attributes
of the divinity branch forth; his unity,
fpirituality, eternity, immutability, omni-
potence, omniprefence, wifdom, juftice,
and goodnefs : thefe again admit of endlefs
fubdivifions, each enlarging with our con-
ceptions,

ceptions, and affording boundlefs objects of contemplation.

PHILOSOPHY, from the moft common appearance in nature, the fall of bodies to the ground, rifes, by a patient *analyfis*, to the great law of gravitation: and having eftablifhed the general principle, fhe extends it over the univerfe, explaining, by *fynthefis*, not only the phænomena of this earth, but the revolutions of the whole planetary fyftem. What a glorious harveft of fcience is thus opened to our view!

———————— Seiz'd in thought
On fancy's wild and roving wing I fail,
From the green borders of the peopled earth,
And the pale moon, her duteous fair attendant ;
From folitary Mars ; from the vaft orb
Of Jupiter, whofe huge gigantic bulk
Dances in ether like the lighteft leaf ;
To the dim verge, the fuburbs of the fyftem,
Where chearlefs Saturn 'midft his wat'ry moons
Girt with a lucid zone, majeftic fits
In gloomy grandeur ; like an exil'd queen
Amongft her weeping handmaids : fearlefs thence
I launch into the tracklefs deeps of fpace,

P   Where,

Where, burning round, ten thousand suns appear,
Of elder beam ; which ask no leave to shine
Of our terrestrial star, nor borrow light
From the proud regent of our scanty day ;
Sons of the morning, first born of creation,
And only less than HIM who marks their track,
And guides their fiery wheels.   Here must I stop,
Or is there aught beyond ? What hand unseen
Impels me onward thro' the glowing orbs
Of habitable nature ; far remote,
To the dread confines of eternal night,
To solitudes of vast unpeopled space,
The deserts of creation, wide and wild ;
Where embryo systems and unkindled suns
Sleep in the womb of chaos ?   Fancy droops,
And thought astonish'd stops her bold career.

MRS. BARBAULD.

BUT if we descend from the scale of
immensity, and consider the opposite extreme of nature, we shall find, that the
gradations of minuteness are infinite, as
those of magnitude ; and that they furnish
subjects of science, less sublime indeed,
but equally inexhaustible. Let us contemplate, for instance, the various classes
of beings, from the monstrous Hippopotamos to the smallest animalcula, which the
microscope has yet discovered, and we shall
perceive

perceive the evidence of this truth. But it will appear ftill more ftriking to us, when we reflect, that life is probably extended far beyond the ken of the moft piercing eye, aided by the beft magnifiers: and life, by analogy, implies, that the animals are endued with limbs, which confift of mufcles, bones, blood-veffels and nerves. Thefe again have their component parts, the divifibility of which feems to admit of no limitation.

ETHICS afford a fpacious field for the growth and cultivation of the choiceft fcions of knowledge. A celebrated Poet remarks, that " the proper ftudy of mankind is man :" and this ftudy originates from the fmalleft beginnings ; enlarges, as the faculties of the mind unfold themfelves, and comprehends, in its progrefs, all the powers and principles which actuate human nature, through the fucceffive ftages of exiftence. In the period of INFANCY, the appetites and fenfes are developed, exercifed and ftrengthened ; they give information of furrounding objects ; excite attention, complacency, furprize, and admiration ;

ration; and the notices they bring, are treafured up in the ftore-houfe of the memory. By the frequent repetition of agreeable impreffions, certain objects become pleafing and familiar to the young fpectator. He diftinguifhes his parents, brothers, and fifters; is uneafy when they are abfent, and delighted to fee them again. Thefe emotions foon conftitute a moral attachment, which reciprocal endearments heighten, gratitude confirms, and habit renders indiffoluble. The amufements of CHILDHOOD, and the active purfuits of YOUTH, add, every day, fome new link to the great chain of focial love. Connections are multiplied, common interefts eftablifhed, mutual dependencies created; and the principles of fympathy, friendfhip, generofity, and benevolence, acquire vigour by exertion, and energy by being uncontrouled. The powers of the underftanding and imagination now expand themfelves; curiofity is awakened, and directed to other objects befides thofe of fenfe; emulation roufes; the thirft of knowledge ftimulates; and the tafte for beauty, in all her varied forms, allures

allures the mind to ftudy and contemplation. The fcenes of nature, at this period
of life, are viewed with peculiar admiration
and delight; and the figns of order, wifdom
and goodnefs, which are every where dif-
cerned, elevate the ideas to the great Parent
of the univerfe, the fountain of being, and
the origin of all perfection. Devotion
glows in the heart; reverence fills the
thoughts; and piety exalts the foul to an
intercourfe with God.

CHERISH, oh! generous youth, the facred flame, thus kindled in thy breaft. *It
will be a light to thy feet, and a lamp to thy
path*; will illuminate thy faculties; fublime
thy virtues; add luftre to thy profperity;
and difpel, with chearing beams, the gloom
of forrow and adverfity.

IN MANHOOD, the purfuit of wealth or
of honour, the duties of marriage, the
cares of a family, and the diverfified offices
of each particular rank and ftation, call
forth into exertion other paffions, or vary

the

the force and direction of thofe already experienced.

Old age at length creeps flowly on:
The generous affections abate in their vigour and warmth ; and anxiety, fufpicion,
fearfulnefs, and the love of money, by infenfible degrees, too often take poffeffion of
the mind. Life increafes in value, the nearer the conclufion of it approaches ; and the
means of enjoyment become moft prized,
when the end, for which they are defigned,
ceafes to be attainable.

Such are generally the weakneffes of de-
clining nature; which though wifdom con-
demns, fhe forbids us not to pity. Happy is
he, who, having ftudied the complicated hiftory of man, knows the fubordination, and
holds the balance of his feveral moral and
intellectual powers: Who can gratify, and
yet regulate his appetites; indulge, but
moderate his paffions; and fetting bounds
to all, maintain inviolate the fupremacy of
reafon.

Thus

THUS it appears, that in Theology, Natural Philofophy, and Ethics, the feeds of knowledge, when cultivated with induf-try and judgment, yield an aftonifhing and inconceivable increafe. The analogy may be extended to various other branches of learning; and the fame important truth will be manifeft in all. Thankful, devout-ly thankful, fhould thofe be, to the Sove-reign Difpenfer of good, who are permit-ted to reap this glorious harveft. For if the acquifition of wealth, or the attainment of power, be juftly deemed fubjects of gra-titude and praife, how much more fo are the riches of fcience, and the empire over nature, which is her dowry?

> He that hath treafures of his own,
> May quit a cottage or a throne ;
> May leave the world,—to dwell alone,
>   Within his fpacious mind.
>   Locke has a foul
>   Wide as the fea,
>   Calm as the night,
>   Bright as the day ;
> There may his vaft ideas play,
> Nor feel a thought confin'd.
>
> WATTS.

P 4   THE

THE exercife and improvement of the
intellectual powers, will probably conftitute no inconfiderable part of the employment and felicity of man, in a future life.
And the prefent ftate may be regarded, as
probationary of the underftanding, as well
as of the heart.   Different circumftances
call forth into action different virtues and
different talents ; and the perfection of the
human character appears to confift in the
number and energy of both, which are
found united in it.   A variety in the purfuits of knowledge, fhould therefore feem
to be moft conducive to the growth and
vigour of our feveral faculties.   For the
activity of the mind, like that of the body,
is increafed by multiplying and diverfifying
its exercifes.   The brawny arms of the
Blackfmith, and the ftrong back of the
Porter, are produced by the long continued exertion of particular mufcles ; but fuch
partial ftrength is not to be compared with
the agility we fee difplayed by thofe, who
have almoft every moving fibre at command.

By

BY an unwearied application to one branch of learning, a man may perhaps become a proficient in it. But the lefs confined his views are, the more eafy and fecure will be the attainment ; becaufe the fciences, whilft they invigorate the under-ftanding, elucidate each other. It is a fact, I believe, not to be controverted, that the moft diftinguifhed Phyficians, Philofophers, and Metaphyficians, in an-cient as well as modern times, have been perfons of general erudition. The names of Hippocrates, Ariftotle, Cicero, Pliny, Bacon, Boyle, Locke, Newton, Hoffman, Haller, Voltaire, Bolingbroke, and Prieft-ley, authenticate the remark, and encou-rage our imitation.

I CANNOT conclude, without noticing the illiberal cenfures we are apt to pafs on thofe purfuits of knowledge, which do not feem immediately fubfervient to the bene-fit of mankind. There are duties which we owe to ourfelves, as well as to fociety ; and he is ufefully and honourably employ-ed, whatever be his ftudy, who is exalting

the

the powers of his own mind, and qualify-
ing himfelf, as a rational being, for the
enjoyments of immortality.   We fhould
remember alfo, that active talents, however acquired, are capable, at the will
of the poffeffor, of being applied to
the moft important purpofes of life.
The profound Mathematician, who has
learned the habits of induftry and accuracy,
can defcend from the inveftigation of the
beauty of ideas, and the harmony of proportions, to improve the ftructure of a
machine, afcertain the variations of the
needle, or calculate a Nautical Almanack.
The Aftronomer, Antiquary, and Critic,
may unite their labours to fix the doubtful
dates of Hiftory, by eftablifhing a juft
Chronology; or to clear the obfcurities,
and to confirm the evidence of the Sacred
Scriptures.   And the Naturalift may drop
the chace of butterflies, and the collection
of infects, to exercife, in his country's fervice, the knowledge which he has attained
of their fpecies, habitudes, and properties.
Not long fince a kind of worms burrowed
in the timber, ufed for fhip-building, in
the

the Royal Dock-Yards of Sweden; and became every year more numerous and deſtructive. The King ſent the celebrated Linnæus from Stockholm, to inquire into the cauſe, and to diſcover a remedy for this growing evil. He found that the worm was produced from a ſmall egg, depoſited by a fly or beetle, in the little roughneſſes on the ſurface of the wood; from whence the worm, as ſoon as it was hatched, began to eat into the ſubſtance of the timber; and after ſometime came out again a fly of the parent kind, leaving behind its little eggs. Linnæus knew that the month of May was the only ſeaſon, in which the fly laid theſe eggs. and he directed all the green timber to be thrown into the ſea, before this ſeaſon commenced, and to be kept under water till the end of it. The flies being thus deprived of their uſual neſts, could not increaſe; and the ſpecies, in a ſhort time, was either deſtroyed, or obliged to migrate to ſome other part of the country *(m)*.

Nor

(m) See Franklin's Obſervations and Experiments.

Nor are thefe obfervations to be confined to fcientific purfuits; for they hold
equally true of fkill in the mechanic
arts. I have been informed that many of
the workmen, who invented and executed
the curious baubles in Mr. Cox's Mufeum,
are now employed, to the greateft advantage, in conftructing vaft engines for the
Collieries at Whitehaven.

COWARDICE and INJUSTICE;
COURAGE and GENEROSITY.

A Little boy was amufing himfelf with
a top, which he whipped with great
expertnefs, on the flags in one of the ftreets
of Manchefter. An older and more lufty
boy, happening to pafs that way, fnatched
up the top, and would have efcaped with
it, if the proprietor had not laid hold of
his coat, and prevented his flight. Remonftrances however were vain; and when
the little boy offered to wreft the top out
of his hand, with more fpirit than ftrength,
he received fo many blows from the plunderer, that he was obliged to defift. Jacobus

cobus was returning from fchool, when he
faw the combatants at a diftance; and he
haftened to them, that he might put an end
to a conteft fo unequal. But before he
arrived, the fenior boy, confcious of his
cowardice and injuftice, and fearing to
engage with one who was his match,
threw down the top, and ran away with
great precipitation. Jacobus related this
little incident to his father, and informed
him, that the boy, whom he had put to
flight, was a terror to all others, inferior
to himfelf in fize and ftrength. Euphronius
liftened to his fon with pleafure; and explained to him the nature of property, and
the bafenefs of depriving another of his
right, either by fraud or violence. He
then repeated the following ftory, to difplay the union of courage with generofity,
and to fhew that it is even below brutality
to attack without being provoked, or to
take undue advantage of the feeblenefs of
an adverfary.

"I REMEMBER a certain perfon inhu-
"manly caft a poor little dog into the den
"of

" of a lion, in full affurance of feeing him
" immediately devoured : But, contrary to
" his expectations, the noble animal not
" only fpared the victim, but foon honour-
" ed him with particular affection. He
" regarded the dog, as an unfortunate
" fellow-prifoner, which, on his part, from
" motives of gratitude, was conftantly
" fawning about his generous lord. They
" long lived together in uninterrupted
" peace and friendfhip ; one watched,
" whilft the other flept. Firft the lion fed,
" and then his humble companion. In a
" word, the magnanimity of the one, and
" the gratitude of the other, had united
" them in the clofeft manner : But a care-
" lefs fervant, forgetting that other crea-
" tures required food as well as himfelf,
" left the two friends twenty-four hours
" without victuals. At laft, recollecting
" his charge, he brought them their ufual
" provifion ; when the dog eagerly catched
" at the firft morfel. But it was at the
" expence of his life : For the angry lion
" inftantly feized his poor companion, and
" crufhed him to death. The perpetration
" of

" of this horrid deed, was inftantly fuc-
" ceeded by a fevere and painful repent-
" ance. The lion's dejection daily in-
" creafed. He refufed his food, with heroic
" obftinacy, and voluntarily famifhed him-
" felf to death."(n)

A CONVERSATION.

Honour and fhame from no condition rife.

PoPE.

SACCHARISSA was about fifteen years
of age. Nature had given her a high
fpirit, and education had foftered it into
pride and haughtinefs. This temper was
difplayed in every little competition which
fhe had with her companions. She could
not brook the leaft oppofition from thofe
whom fhe regarded as her inferiors ; and if
they did not inftantly fubmit to her incli-
nation, fhe affumed all her airs of dignity,
and treated them with the moft fupercilious
contempt.

(n) See Count Teffin's Letters to the Prince Royal of
Sweden, Vol. I. p. 194.

contempt. She domineered over her father's fervants, always commanding their
good offices with the voice of authority;
and difdaining the gentler language of requeft. Euphronius was walking with her
yefterday, when the gardener brought her a
nofegay, which fhe had ordered him to collect. You blockhead! fhe cried, as he delivered it to her, what ftrange flowers have you
chofen, and how aukwardly have you put
them together! Blame not the man with
fo much harfhnefs, faid Euphronius, becaufe his tafte is different from yours! He
meant to pleafe you, and his good intention merits your thanks, and not your cenfure. Thanks! replied Sacchariffa, fcorn-
fully. He is paid for his fervices, and it
is his duty to perform them. And if he do
perform them, he acquits himfelf of his
duty, returned Euphronius. The obligation is fulfilled on his fide, and you have
no more right to upbraid him for executing
your orders according to his beft ability,
than he has to claim from your father
more wages than were covenanted to be
given him. But he is a poor dependent,
faid

faid Sacchariffa, and earns a livelihood by
his daily labour. That livelihood, anfwered Euphronius, is the juft price of his labour ; and if he receive nothing farther
from your hands, the account is balanced
between you. But a generous perfon com-
paffionates the lot of thofe, who are ne-
ceffitated to toil for his benefit or gratification. He lightens their burthens ; treats
them with kindnefs and affection ; ftudies
to promote their intereft and happinefs ;
and as much as poffible conceals from them
their fervitude, and his fuperiority. The
diftinctions of rank and fortune he regards
as accidental ; and though the circumftances of life require that there fhould be
hewers of wood, and drawers of water, yet
he forgets not that mankind are by nature
equal ; all being the offspring of God, the
fubjects of his moral government, and
joint heirs of immortality. A conduct
directed by fuch principles, gives a mafter
claims which no money can purchafe, no
labour can repay. His affection can only
be compenfated by love ; his kindnefs by

Q   gratitude ;

gratitude; and his cordiality by the fervice of the heart.

SACCHARISSA heard thefe remonftrances with aftonifhment; and was fhocked at the idea of being degraded to an equality with her father's domeftics. Euphronius perceived the emotions of her mind; and thus continued the converfation. In the form and ftructure of their bodies, you muft acknowledge that they bear a perfect refemblance to you. Perhaps you will confefs alfo that they excel you in health, ftrength, and agility. They can endure the heats of fummer, and the rigours of winter; the cravings of hunger, and the fatigues of labour; whilft you fhiver with the fummer's breeze, obey every call of appetite, and are incapable of toil or hardfhip. Thus your more elevated ftation increafes your wants, and leffens your perfonal abilities to fupply them : And you are a *dependant* on the induftry and fkill of thoufands for your food, raiment, and habitation. Sacchariffa ftartled at the word *dependant*; and urged Euphronius to explain

plain his meaning. Remember then, said he, that if I mortify your pride, it is in compliance with your own requeſt. You are no ſtranger to the compoſition of bread; but it is probable that you never conſidered how much art and labour are neceſſary to furniſh you with this plain and common article of diet. The farmer and his hinds ſow the grain; reap it when ripe; gather it into the barn; threſh it; and ſeparate the chaff from the wheat. Theſe operations require the plough, the harrow, the ſickle, the cart, the flail, and the winnower; inſtruments which give employment to numberleſs hands, in the workmanſhip or materials of them. Take the plough for an example. It conſiſts of iron and wood. Iron is dug out of the bowels of the earth, and perhaps tranſported to us from Sweden or America. The ore of it is to be calcined, fuſed, caſt, and wrought into bars, before the metal is fitted for the artiſt, who is to faſhion it. Such proceſſes cannot be carried on without furnaces, bellows, charcoal, and a variety of tools and conveniences. Theſe again admit of further ſub-

diviſion;

divifion; and you fee miners, fhipwrights, failors, fmelters, coakers, mafons, blackfmiths, &c. &c. unite their labours to complete the ploughfhare.

THE other part of the plough is generally made of the wood of the afh and of the oak; and employs the planter, feller, fawyer, and carpenter; befides all the artificers who furnifh them with their feveral implements. When the wheat is feparated from the chaff, it is put into facks, and fent to the mill. The facks are manufactured of hemp, which paffes through a multiplicity of hands, before it reaches the weaver; whofe loom, fhuttle, and reed, are again the productions of a variety of artifts. The fame obfervation is applicable to the mill; the machinery of which confifts of fo many parts, that it would be tedious to attempt the enumeration of them.

THE flour being thus provided, at the expence of fo much time, fkill and induftry, it muft be mixed with water, yeaft, and

and falt, and then baked in the oven.
Yeaft prefuppofes fermentation, and all
the antecedents neceffary to effect it. Salt
is either obtained from fea-water, or fprings
of brine; or it is found in a cryftalline
form in the bowels of the earth. You
have been a witnefs, at Northwich, to the
many operations which it undergoes; and
to the number of men who are occupied in
the preparation of it. The baker muft be
furnifhed with a fhovel, with faggots, and
with an oven; and each of thefe afford
employment to different fpecies of art and
induftry.

Euphronius paufed here, and obferved
with pleafure, that Sacchariffa appeared to
be impreffed by what he had delivered.
You are fenfible, I hope, continued he, of
the obligations which you owe to thoufands, for every morfel of bread that you
eat. Extend your reflections farther, and
confider, in the fame manner, the·other
articles of your food, the conveniences of
your dwelling, and all the various parts of
your drefs; and you will find that the la-

Q 3   bour

bour beftowed upon you, exceeds all computation *(o)*.

You have exalted me, in my own eftimation, faid Sacchariffa jocularly, by fhewing that fuch multitudes are employed in my fervice. And your leffon, fo far from teaching humility, feems rather to juftify what you term pride.

Euphronius replied, that this was a ftrange perverfion of his argument : for if a dependence on the labour and good offices of others be a real exaltation, we have moft reafon for pride in childhood, ficknefs, or in a ftate of idiocy. Under fuch circumftances, we receive the higheft benefit from the community, without *degrading* ourfelves by any perfonal fervices in return. Befides, in the prefent improved ftate of focial life, the loweft mechanic, as well as the richeft citizen, may boaft that thoufands of his fellow-creatures are employed
for

(o) A pin, trifling as the value of it may be deemed, generally paffes through eighteen hands before it is completed. See Smith on the Caufes of the Wealth of Nations.

for him; and that the accommodations of his humble cottage have coſt more toil and induſtry, than the palaces of many a monarch on the coaſt of Africa.

The eſtate of your father, Sacchariſſa, was honourably acquired by your anceſtor, Lyſander. Your ſubſiſtence and enjoyments, therefore, are the price of his labour. But the ſubſiſtence and enjoyments of your gardener are the price of his own. With ſkill, and diligence, he cultivates the ſoil, and raiſes the fruits of the earth You purchaſe them with the earnings of your grandſire; and conſume them in ſloth and diſſipation. Compare his condition with yours, in this point of light, and then determine which is moſt reſpectable!

Such reflections were ſtrange and novel to Sacchariſſa. She continued muſing for ſome time; but, at length, renewed the converſation, by aſking whether ſhe might not reaſonably pride herſelf on the ſuperiority over others in knowledge and power,

which

which education, rank, and fortune had given her?

KNOWLEDGE, replied Euphronius, is intrinfically valuable, as it elevates the mind, and qualifies us for higher degrees of felicity, both in the prefent, and in a future life. But with refpect to others, it affords no claim of diftinction, unlefs it be applied to their emolument. *Power*, abftractedly confidered, is of little eftimation; and may either dignify or degrade the poffeffor. If you wifh to derive honour from it, be careful to render it fubfervient to the happinefs of all around you; and enjoy with gratitude, not with affected fuperiority, the exalted privilege of doing good. Has your mind been cultivated by a liberal education; Be thankful to God, and to your parents; but remember, with humility, how far your ignorance exceeds your knowledge.

IT is not confiftent with wifdom either to over-rate our own attainments, or to undervalue thofe of others. The gardener, whom

whom you juft now treated with fuch contempt, is a man of fcience, though unacquainted with any branch of the *Belles Lettres*. He is verfed in the nature of foils, the variety of feeds, the habitudes of plants, the culture of trees, the multiplication of flowers, and in all that relates to the curious and important fyftem of vegetable life. The acquifition and daily application of this ufeful knowledge, exercifes and invigorates the powers of his underftanding; and he learns to compare, to difcriminate, to reafon, and to judge with no lefs accuracy than the logician, the ftatefman, the divine, or the philofopher. Euphronius was proceeding to extend the obfervation to mechanics and artifts; but he was interrupted by a little incident, not worth relating, which put an end to the converfation.

IRASCIBILITY and FALSE HONOUR.

TWO cocks, who were traverfing their refpective dunghills with all the pride
of

of confcious dignity, happened to crow
very loudly at the fame time. Each heard
with indignation the voice of the other,
becaufe each deemed it an infult and a
challenge; and honour required of both
that an affront fo grofs fhould be revenged.
They defcended from their dunghills, and
with majeftic fteps and briftling plumage
met together. The engagement foon began, the match was equal, and it was un-
certain to which fide victory inclined. A
game cock, cooped in a pen, beheld the
combatants, with an ardent defire to
fhare the glories of the field. By accident
the door of his pen had been left unfaften-
ed; he pufhed it open, and ran eagerly to
mingle in the battle. Being much fuperi-
or to the dunghill cocks, in agility and
ftrength, he quickly routed and put them
both to flight. And he exulted in the
mighty atchievement, by crowing, ftrut-
ting, and clapping his wings. The ftrength
and courage however derived from the
infamous arts of feeding, are but of fhort
duration. In a few hours he was obferved
to droop, and his antagonifts, now returning

ing to the attack, found him feeble, pufil-
lanimous, and fo eafy a conqueft, that he
fell on the firft onfet.

In the dunghill cocks you may view the
picture of thofe, who ftile themfelves *men
of honour*; and the game cock will remind
you of many a rakifh youth, who inflamed
with wine, iffues from the tavern to engage
in the firft brawl he meets with.   His
ftrength and courage are but the tranfient
effects of liquor, and being foon exhaufted,
he is made to feel feverely the folly and
rafhnefs of his conduct.

I have heard it fuggefted, that valour
depends intirely on the ftate of the bodily
organs, *(p)* and that a coward may be
dieted into a hero, and a hero into a
coward.   Though this opinion feems to be
chimerical, yet it muft be acknowledged,
that the effects of regimen are very aftonifhing

(p) Pusillanimity is a characteriftic of the inhabitants
of the Eaft Indies; and it is faid, that they generally take
opium before any arduous and dangerous enterprife, to give
them vigour and courage.

ing. Dry ftimulating food, and evacuations diminifh the weight of the body, by wafting the fat, and leffening the liver; and they increafe the weight of the heart, by augmenting the quantity and motion of the blood.

A GAME cock, in ten days, is brought to his athletic ftate, and prepared for fighting. If the food, evacuations, and exercife, be continued longer, the ftrength, courage, and activity of the cock will be impaired; owing perhaps to the lofs of weight falling at laft on the heart, blood, and mufcles. *(q)*

IT is known from experience, that a cock does not remain in his athletic ftate above twenty-four hours; and that he changes very much for the worfe in twelve hours. When he is in the higheft vigour, his head is of a glowing red colour, his neck large, and his thigh thick, and firm. The fucceeding day his complexion is lefs glowing, his neck thinner, and his thigh
fofter;

(q) See Dr. Robinfon on the Food and Difcharges of the Body.

foft'er; and the third day his thigh will be very foft and flaccid. Four game cocks, reduced to their athletic weights, were killed, and found to be very full of blood, with large hearts, large mufcles, and no fat.

THE TIGER AND THE ELEPHANT

True Courage exerted in repelling, not in offering Injuries.

IN one of the Deferts of Africa, a tiger of uncommon fize, agility, and fierce-nefs, committed the moft dreadful ravages. He attacked every animal he met with, and was never fatiated with blood and flaughter. Refiftance ferved only to in-creafe his ferocity, and paffive timidity to multiply his victims. When the foreft afforded him no prey, he lurked near a fountain of water, and feized, in quick fucceffion, and with indifcriminate cruelty, the various beafts that came to drink. It happened that an elephant ftopped to quench his thirft at the ftream, whilft
the

the tiger lay concealed in the adjoining thicket.

THE fight of a creature fo ftupendous, rather incited than reftrained his rapacity. He compared his own agility with the unweildy bulk of the elephant; and trufting that he fhould find him as unfit to fight, as to fly, he bounded towards him, and fnatched, with open jaws, at his probofcis.   The elephant inftantly contracted it, with great prefence of mind; and receiving the furious beaft on his tufks, toffed him up a confiderable height into the air. Stunned with his fall, the tiger lay motionlefs fome time; and the generous elephant, difdaining revenge, left him to recover from his bruifes.   When the tiger came to himfelf, (like the aggreffor in every quarrel) he was enraged at the repulfe; and purfuing his injured and peaceable adverfary, he again affailed him, with redoubled violence.   The refentment of the elephant was now roufed: he wounded the tiger with his tufks, and then beat him to death with his trunk.

DOES

Does the ferocity of the tiger merit the honourable appellation of courage ? Or will you not rather apply that epithet to the calm intrepidity of the inoffensive elephant ? The moral diftinction is of confiderable importance; and if it be clearly underftood, you will deteft the brutal character of an Achilles, whether you meet with it in the page of hiftory, or in the tranfactions of life.

Impiger, iracundus, inexorabilis, acer;
Jura neget fibi nata, nihil non arroget
    armis. (r)

The PARASITE PLANT.

THERE is a plant in the Weft Indies, called the *Caraguata,* which clings round the tree that is neareft to its root, and foon gains the afcendant, covers the branches with a foreign verdure, robs them of nourifhment, and at laft deftroys it fupporter.

THE

(r) Hor. de Art Poet. V. 121.

THE diftinguifhing charaċters of the Caraguata are not confined to the vegetable kingdom, nor peculiar to any climate. They are found in the human fpecies, and may be obferved in every country. The monarch, who exalts his own power, by the debafement of the people from whom it is derived; the ftatefman who builds his greatnefs on the ruin of his country; and the profligate youth, whofe extravagance reduces to penury a too indulgent father; each belongs to the clafs of the *Caraguata*.

IMMORTALITY.

EUPHRONIUS was fometimes vifited, at Hart-hill, by his friend Hiero; the chearful, the pious, and the benevolent Hiero; whofe life was almoft equally divided between the ftudy of knowledge, the exercifes of virtue, and the enjoyments of devout contemplation. One evening he retired from the table at an early hour; and Julius who happened to be prefent, and to be looking through the window,

saw

faw him foon afterwards, open a little gate, at the end of the garden, and direct his courfe towards a fequeftered path, which he loved to frequent. Curiofity incited him to follow the pious philofopher; and, unperceived by Hiero, he placed himfelf behind the ftump of a tree, fufficiently near, to mark his words and geftures. For Hiero was accuftomed to *think aloud* in his folitary walks, and was now repeating the following lines.

" At this ftill hour the felf-collected foul
" Turns inward, and beholds a ftranger there
" Of high defcent, and more than mortal rank;
" An embryo GOD; a fpark of fire divine,
" Which muft burn on for ages, when the fun
" (Fair tranfitory creature of a day!)
" Has clos'd his golden eye, and wrapt in fhades
" Forgets his wonted journey thro' the eaft. *(s)*

HERE he paufed; and remained fome time buried in profound reflection. Then rifing with emotion from his feat, forgive, he cried, Oh! gracious heaven, the impious fear, which frailty hath fuggefted to my
R   mind.

(s) Mrs. Barbauld's Poems.

mind. Reafon difclaims the gloomy terrors
of annihilation, and bids afpiring hope direct her views to immortality. The folemn
filence which reigns around me, and which
fancy painted as the image of *death*, is but
the *fleep* of animated nature. Soon the
chearing beams of light will burft, with
refplendent glory, from the eaft ; and the
dawning day will awaken the creatures of
God, to action and enjoyment. But the
inferior ranks of beings, feem to be incapable of thofe progreffive improvements,
which characterife the human kind. Beafts,
birds, and infects fill their refpective
fpheres, with unvaried equality ; and generation fucceeds to generation without the
advancement of a fingle fpecies in the
fcale of excellence.

THE fhort period of their lives appears
adequate to the perfection, which they
are qualified to attain; and the fovereign
of the univerfe hath proclaimed to them
his law, *Hitherto fhall ye go and no farther.*
But man is never ftationary, never fatisfied with the acquifitions which he makes.
The

The deepeft draughts of knowledge ferve only to increafe his thirft; exaltation in virtue but inflames his ambition; and his foaring fpirit urges onward; ever approaching to, yet ever infinitely diftant from the ftandard of perfection.

HIERO again paufed; and viewing with earneft attention the fpangled concave of heaven, he thus addreffed himfelf to the ftars, at the fame time purfuing his walk.

> Ye citadels of light,
> Perhaps my future home, from whence the foul
> Revolving periods paft, may oft look back,
> With recollected tendernefs, on all
> The various bufy fcenes fhe left below,
> Its deep laid projects and its ftrange events,
> As on fome fond and doting tale that footh'd
> Her infant hours. —— *(t)*

HE was now almoft out of hearing, and Julius left his covert to follow him. But finding it impoffible to conceal himfelf, he accofted the philofopher, and honeftly confeffed that he had been liftening to his

foliloquy.

(t) Mrs. Barbauld's Poems.

foliloquy. He apologifed for the intrufion; and intreated Hiero to purfue his meditations, without regard to his prefence. Happy fhall I think myfelf, continued he, if you can convince me of my *title* to immortality.

HAVE you difcovered any *flaw* in your *title*, replied Hiero, with his ufual complacency, that you thus exprefs yourfelf with doubt concerning fo invaluable a reverfion? No *evidence*, that I am acquainted with, has yet been adduced by the moft fubtle fceptic againft a future ftate. So that the probability of it is, at the firft view, equal to its improbability. And if only a fingle argument can be advanced in favour of it, the fcale on that fide will inftantly preponderate. Your ignorance of the mode of exiftence in another world, and of the tranfition by death, from this life to the next, can have no weight in the balance. For ignorance is neither a foundation of faith, nor of incredulity; and if we reafon from it, we are fure to be involved in error. Shew an acorn to a
Hottentot,

Hottentot, or wild Arab, who has never travelled beyond his own fandy defarts; and inform him that it will become a lofty tree, with fpreading branches: the account will feem marvellous to his untutored mind; and he may fufpend his belief of it, but cannot reject it as a falfhood.

THE condition of a child before its birth, bears very little analogy to the ftate of man in his maturity: and if you can fuppofe a perfon to be ignorant that the one is preparatory to the other, fuch ignorance would be no authority for the denial of the fact.

But there are many pofitive arguments, on which we may juftly ground our conviction of a future life. The ardent defire and expectation of it, and the dread of annihilation, which are common to all mankind, may furely be regarded as prefumptions in favour of immortality. Defire, whether we judge from analogy, or from the moral attributes of God, feems to imply the reality of its object; and the belief of

R 3   this

this reality, which has prevailed in almoſt e-
very age, and nation, muſt either have ariſen
from ſome divine revelation, or from its
conſonancy to the univerſal principles of
human reaſon. *(u)*

CONSCIENCE alſo, by ſuggeſting the
idea of a future and ſolemn tribunal, confirms the expectation of another life. The
rewards of virtue, and the puniſhments of
vice, have generally their commencement
here; but we look to the world that is to
come for their completion.

MERIT, and demerit, however, do not
always meet with proportionate rewards,
or puniſhments, in the preſent ſtate. Suf-
fering

(u) M. Michaelis, in his learned Diſſertation on the reciprocal Influence of Language and Opinions, hath obſerved
that the Greeks made uſe of the ſame word (ΨΥ´ΧΗ.
1. PAPILIO. 2. ANIMA.) for the SOUL, which in its primary
ſignification expreſſes a BUTTERFLY. For a Butterfly is only
a caterpillar, that changes its form without dying, and bears
therein a ſimilitude to the Soul; which continues to exiſt in its
new ſtate, after the diſſolution of the body. It was for this
reaſon that the Greeks firſt repreſented the Soul hieroglyphical-
ly, under the form of a butterfly; and afterwards proceeded to
give it the very name of that inſect.

fering virtue, and triumphant vice are irregularities, which we daily obferve in the difpenfations of Providence; and they evidently point out an hereafter, when the Deity will vindicate the wifdom, benevolence, and equity of his adminiftration.

It appears to be an inconfiftency that death fhould be the final event of life; and that the period of exiftence fhould be clofed with fuffering. Pain is often fubfervient to pleafure; and the evils which we undergo, for the moft part, contribute to our improvement and perfection. Shall the laft pang therefore that we experience, and the greateft in our apprehenfions, prove the eternal extinction of our being? Rather, Julius, let us fuppofe that our paffage into another world refembles our birth into this; that both are neceffarily attended with fome degree of pain; and that the maturity of the human is but the infancy of the heavenly life.

I would banifh all *fuppofition*, however probable, faid Julius; and acknowledge

R 4   the

the validity of no arguments fhort of *demonftration*.

BANISH then your pretenfions to Philofophy, replied Hiero, and avow a general
fcepticifm! For how few are the truths
which admit of *demonftration?* Probability
is almoft the univerfal foundation of our
reafoning; and the wifeft men are governed by it, both in their fpeculations, and in
the moft interefting tranfactions of life.
The nature and force of evidence neceffarily vary with its objects; and whatever be
our inquiries or purfuits, we can expect
only that kind and degree of it, which
they are capable of affording. But in
phyfical refearches we hefitate not to yield
our affent to a theory, that folves the phe-
nomena which it profeffes to explain:
And affent is heightened into conviction,
when it appears that numerous facts confirm, and no one oppofes it. But in
what does the *theory of a future ftate* differ
from that of Magnetifm or of Gravitation,
except in its tranfcendent importance to
mankind?

JULIUS

JULIUS made no reply. The night was far advanced; and Hiero, impatient to enjoy in folitude his own reflections, haftened back to his apartment at Hart-Hill.

The TAME GEESE and WILD GEESE.

TWO geefe ftrayed from a farm yard, in the fens of Lincolnfhire, and fwam down a canal to a large morafs, which afforded them an extenfive range and plenty of food. A flock of wild geefe frequently reforted to this morafs; and though at firft they were fhy, and would not fuffer the tame ones to join them, by degrees they became well acquainted, and affociated freely together. One evening their cackling reached the ears of a fox, that was prowling at no great diftance from the morafs. The artful plunderer directed his courfe through a wood on the borders of it, and was within a few yards of his prey, before any of the geefe perceived him. But the alarm was given,

juft

just as he was springing upon them; and
the whole flock instantly ascended into the
air, with loud and dissonant cries. The
wild geese winged their flight into the
higher regions, and were seen no more;
but the two tame ones, unused to soar,
and habituated to receive protection without any exertion of their own powers, soon
dropped down, and became succeffively
the victims of the fox.

THE faculties of every animal are impaired by disuse, and strengthened by exer-
cise.   And in man, the energy and ver-
satility of the mind depend upon action,
no less than the vigour and agility of the
body.

BEAUTY AND DEFORMITY.

A YOUTH, who lived in the country,
and who had not acquired, either by
reading or conversation, any knowledge of
the animals which inhabit foreign regions,
came to Manchester, to see an exhibition
of

of wild beafts. The fize and figure of the
elephant ftruck him with awe ; and he
viewed the rhinoceros with aftonifhment.
But his attention was foon withdrawn from
thefe animals, and directed to another, of
the moft elegant and beautiful form; and
he ftood contemplating with filent admiration the gloffy fmoothnefs of his hair ; the
blacknefs and regularity of the ftreaks with
which he was marked ; the fymmetry of
his limbs; and above all, the placid fweetnefs of his countenance. What is the name
of this lovely animal, faid he to the keeper,
which you have placed near one of the
uglieft beafts in your collection, as if you
meant to contraft beauty with deformity ?
Beware, young man, replied the keeper,
of being fo eafily captivated with external
appearance. The animal, which you admire, is called a tiger, and notwithftanding
the meeknefs of his looks, he is fierce and
favage beyond defcription. I can neither
terrify him by correction, nor tame him
by indulgence. But the other beaft, which
you defpife, is in the higheft degree docile,
affectionate, and ufeful. For the benefit

of

of man, he traverfes the fandy defarts of
Arabia, where drink and pafture are feldom
to be found; and will continue fix or feven
days without fuftenance, yet ftill patient of
labour. His hair is manufactured into
cloathing; his flefh is deemed wholefome
nourifhment; and the milk of the female
is much valued by the Arabs. The camel
therefore, for fuch is the name given to this
animal, is more worthy of your admiration
than the tiger; notwithftanding the inele-
gance of his make, and the two bunches upon
his back. For mere external beauty is of
little eftimation; and deformity, when affociated with amiable difpofitions and ufeful qualities, does not preclude our refpect
and approbation.

PHILOSOPHICAL ATTENTION AND SAGACITY.

AN attentive and inquifitive mind often derives very important inftruction
from appearances and events, which the
generality of mankind regard as trivial and
infignificant.

infignificant. Permit me, Alexis, to offer to you a few examples, of the truth of this obfervation. You have frequently remarked, and perhaps admired the volubility and luftre of the globules of rain, that lie upon the leaves of colewort, and of other vegetables; but I dare fay, you have never taken the trouble of infpecting them narrowly. Mr. Melville, a young philofopher of uncommon genius, was ftruck with the phenomenon, and applied his attention to the inveftigation of it. He difcovered that the luftre of the drop is owing to a copious reflection of light, from the flattened part of its furface, contiguous to the plant ; and that when the drop rolls over a part, which has been wetted, it inftantly lofes all its brightnefs, the green leaf being feen through it. From thefe two obfervations he concludes, that the drop does not really *touch* the plant, whilft it retains a mercurial appearance, but is fufpended by the force of a repulfive power. For there could not be any copious reflection of white light, from its under furface, unlefs there was a real interval between it and the plant.

plant. And if no contact be suppofed, it is eafy to account for the wonderful volubility of the drop, and why no traces of moifture are left wherever it rolls.

FROM this reafoning we may conclude, that when a polifhed needle is made to fwim on water, it does not touch the water, but forms around it, by a repulfive power, a bed, whofe concavity is much larger than the bulk of the needle. And this affords a much better explanation of the fact, than the common one, deduced from the tenacity of the water. For the needle may be well conceived to fwim upon a fluid lighter than itfelf, fince the quantity of water thus difplaced, by repulfion, muft be equal to the weight of it. And this inftance leads us to a juft and neceffary correction of the hydroftatical law, that the *whole fwimming body is equal in weight to a quantity of the fluid, whofe bulk is equal to that of the part immerfed.* For it fhould be expreffed, that *the weight of the fwimming body is equal to that of the weight, of the quantity of fluid difplaced by it.*

A VERY

A very ingenious friend of mine, during his refidence at the univerfity, undertook a courfe of experiments, to afcertain the heat or cold produced by the folution of certain fubftances in fpirit of wine. Whenever he withdrew the thermometer from the fpirit, and fufpended it in the air, he uniformly obferved, that the mercury funk two or three degrees, although the fpirit of wine, in which the inftrument had been immerfed, was even colder than the furrounding atmofphere. This fact he communicated to the profeffor of chemiftry; who immediately fufpected, that *fluids by evaporation generate cold*; an hypothefis, which he afterwards verified by a variety of beautiful, and decifive trials.

When Sir John Pringle and Dr. Franklin were travelling together in Holland, they remarked, that the track-fchuyt, or barge, in one of the ftages, moved flower than ufual, and inquired the reafon of it. The boatman informed them, that it had been a dry feafon, and that the water was low in the canal. He was afked, if the

water

water was fo low that the boat touched the muddy bottom of the canal; to which he anfwered in the negative, adding, however, that the difference in the quantity of water, was fufficient to render the draught more difficult to the horfe. The travellers, at firft, were at a lofs to conceive, how the depth of the water could affect the motion of the boat, provided that it fwam clear of the bottom. But Dr. Franklin, having fatisfied himfelf of the truth of the boatman's obfervation, began to confider it attentively; and endeavoured to account for it in the following manner. The barge, in proceeding along the canal, muft regularly difplace a body of water, equal in bulk to the fpace which fhe occupies ; and the water fo removed muft pafs underneath, and on each fide of her. Hence if the paffage, under her bottom, be ftraitned by the fhallows, more of the water muft pafs by her fides, and with greater velocity, which will retard her courfe, becaufe fhe moves the contrary way. The water, alfo, becoming lower behind than before the boat, fhe will be preffed back by the weight of its

difference

difference in height ; and her paffage will be obftructed by having that weight conftantly to overcome.

However fatisfactory this reafoning might appear to be, Dr. Franklin determined to afcertain the truth of it by experiment ; deeming the fubject of confiderable importance to the inhabitants of a country, in which fo many projects for navigable canals have been adopted. And he concludes, from many well concerted trials, the relation of which would now be tedious to you, that if four men or horfes be required to draw a boat, in *deep water*, four leagues in four hours ; five will be neceffary to draw the boat, the fame diftance in the fame time, in *fhallow water*.

I shall give you one inftance more of the advantages of fagacious attention, which may, perhaps, be more amufing to you, than thofe which I have recited.

A playful boy, whofe bufinefs it was to open and clofe alternately, the commu-

S nication

nication between the boiler and the cylin-
der of a fire engine, perceived that this
trouble might readily be faved.   Whenever, therefore, he wifhed to be at liberty
to divert himfelf with his companions, he
tied a ftring from the handle of the valve,
which formed the communication, to another part of the machine that was in motion ; and the valve then performed its office
without affiftance.   The boy's idlenefs being remarked, his contrivance foon became
known, and the improvement is now a-
dopted in every fire engine.

The JOLLY FELLOW.

RODERIC was a young man who had
neglected the cultivation of his underftanding, and had made an early facrifice
of knowledge to merriment.   He could
fing a jovial fong, and tell a ftory admi-
rably ; for he defpifed truth when it inter-
fered with the embellifhments of humour.
His fociety was courted by the gay and
the diffipated ; and whenever he exerted
his

his talents, he fet the *table in a roar*.
But Roderic was fubject to fudden revolutions of mind. At a convivial meeting,
one day, he had been more than ufually
lively and facetious. The Champagne
went brifkly round, and bottle after bottle,
in quick fucceffion, was emptied and caft
afide. All at once he became penfive;
his countenance fell; his eyes were fixed;
and he feemed loft in meditation. The
company rallied him, and demanded the
caufe of fuch an unexpected tranfition from
jollity to gloom. Certain ftrange ideas,
faid he, have obtruded themfelves upon
me; and I am fhocked to perceive how
exactly I refemble the bottle of Champagne
that is before us. The anfwer was a
myftery. After a fhort paufe he unravelled
it. Like this bottle, continued he, I am
only fparkling and frothy; the fource of
exhilaration, but not of fatisfaction. Sick-
nefs or misfortune, the ftorms of life, may
four my wit, or flatten my fpirits; time
will inevitably exhauft them, and I fhall
then be put away with contempt, as an
empty veffel, of no intrinfic value.

THE

THE DUNGHILL COCK.

OBSERVE that cock, said the wealthy and plodding Apicius! He has found a way into my Granary, and though he ſtands upon a large heap of corn, where he may gratify all his wants without pains or trouble, yet he *ſcrapes* with as much eagerneſs as if he were earning his ſcanty pittance on the dunghill. And is not his maſter, anſwered I, daily chargeable with the like folly, though he boaſts of reaſon, and ridicules the undiſtinguiſhing operations of inſtinct. Providence has furniſhed him with abundance, but he toils with anxiety for more. He impatiently ſearches tor new treaſures, whilſt he ſhould be enjoying thoſe which he poſſeſſes: And in the midſt of affluence he ſuffers the evils of penury.

PERSECU-

ARAM was fitting at the door of
his tent, under the fhade of his fig-
tree; when it came to pafs that a man,
ftricken with years bearing his ftaff in his
hand, journeyed that way. And it was
noon day. And Aram faid unto the
ftranger, pafs not by, I pray thee, but
come in, and wafh thy feet, and tarry here
until the evening; for thou art ftricken
with years, and the heat overcometh thee.
And the ftranger left his ftaff at the door,
and entered into the tent of Aram. And
he refted himfelf; and Aram fet before him
bread, and cakes of fine meal baked upon
the hearth. And Aram bleffed the bread,
calling upon the name of the Lord. But
the ftranger did eat, and refufed to pray
unto the Moft High; faying, thy Lord is
not the God of my fathers; why therefore
fhould I prefent my vows unto him? And
Aram's wrath was kindled: and he called
his fervants: and they beat the ftranger, and

S 3   drove

drove him into the wildernefs. Now in
the evening, Aram lifted up his voice unto
the Lord, and prayed unto him; and the
Lord faid Aram, where is the ftranger
that fojourned this day with thee? And
Aram anfwered and faid, behold O! Lord
he ate of thy bread, and would not offer
unto thee his prayers and thanksgivings.
Therefore did I chaftife him, and drive
him from before me into the wildernefs.
And the Lord faid unto Aram, who hath
made thee a judge between me and him?
Have not I borne with thine iniquities, and
winked at thy backflidings; and fhalt thou
be fevere with thy brcther, to mark his
errors, and to punifh his perverfenefs?
Arife and follow the ftranger; and carry
with thee oil and wine, and anoint his
bruifes, and fpeak kindly unto him. For
I, the Lord thy God, am a jealous God, and
judgment belongeth alone unto me. Vain
is thine oblation of thankfgiving without a
lowly heart. As a bulrufh thou mayeft
bow down thine head, and lift up thy
voice like a trumpet, but thou obeyeft not
the ordinance of thy God, if thy worfhip
be

be for ſtrife and debate. Behold the ſacri-
fice that I have choſen, is it not to undo
the heavy burdens; to let the opreſſed go
free; and to break every yoke? To deal
thy bread to the hungry; and to bring the
poor, that are caſt out, to thy houſe? And
Aram trembled before the preſence of
God. And he aroſe; and put on ſackcloth
and aſhes; and went out into the wilder-
neſs, to do as the Lord had commanded
him. *(x)*

TRUTH NEVER IMPRESSES THE MIND MORE
FORCIBLY, THAN WHEN SUGGESTED BY A
JUST AND STRIKING ANALOGY.

WHEN Charles the V. had reſigned
the ſceptre of Spain, and the imperial crown of Germany, he retired to
the monaſtery of St. Juſtus, near the city
of Placentia in Eſtremadura. It was ſeat-

S 4   ed

(x) This parable is an imitation of one compoſed by Dr.
Franklin; if that may be called an imitation which was written without a ſight, and from a very imperfect account of
the original. Mr. *Dodſley,* has inſerted the preſent piece in the
Annual Regiſter for 1777; but it has here undergone ſome al-
terations.

ed in a vale, of no great extent, watered
by a fmall brook, and furrounded by rifing
grounds, covered with lofty trees. From
the nature of the foil, as well as the tem-
perature of the climate, it was efteemed
the moft healthful and delicious fituation
in Spain. Here he cultivated, with his
own hands, the plants in his garden; and
fometimes he rode out to a neighbouring
wood, on a little horfe, attended only by
a fingle fervant on foot. When his in-
firmities confined him to his apartment,
and deprived him of thefe more active re-
creations, he either admitted a few gentlemen,. who refided near the monaftery,
to vifit him, and entertained them fami-
liarly at his own table; or he employed himfelf in ftudying mechanical principles, and in forming works of mecha-
nifm, of which he had always been remarkably fond, and to which his genius
was peculiarly turned. He was extremely
curious with regard to the conftruction of
clocks and watches; and having found,
after repeated trials, that he could not
bring any two of them to go exactly alike,
he

he reflected, with a mixture of furprife
as well as regret, on his own folly, (as
he might also on his cruelty and injuftice)
in having exerted himfelf with fo much
zeal and perfeverance in the more vain attempt of bringing mankind to a uniformity
of fentiment, concerning the doctrines of
religion. *(y)* Happy would it have been
for Europe, if this juft and ftriking analogy
had occurred to the monarch during the
plenitude of his power! And happy might
it now prove, if allowed to operate againft
the fpirit of bigotry and perfecution, which
ftill actuates many individuals, and even
large communities.

The PEDLAR and his ASS.

IT was noon day, and the fun fhone
intenfely bright, when a Pedlar, driving
his Afs laden with the choiceft Burflem
ware, ftopped upon Delamere foreft to
tafte fome refrefhment. He fat down upon
the turf, and after confuming the provifions

in

(y) See Robertfon's Hiftory of Charles V.

in his fatchel, emptied his dram bottle, and then compofed himfelf to fleep. But the Afs, who had travelled many a wearifome mile without tafting a morfel of food, re-mained muzzled by his fide, wiftfully viewing the bloffoms of furze which grew in great abundance around them. Fatigue and heat however overpowered the fenfa-tions of hunger, and drowfinefs ftole upon him. He' kneeled down, and doubling his legs under him, refted upon his belly in fuch a pofition that each of the panniers which he carried touched the ground, and was fecurely fupported by it. But his flumbers were of fhort duration. An angry hornet, whofe neft had been that morning deftroyed, perched upon his back, and ftung him to the quick. Roufed by the fmart he fuddenly fprung up, and by this violent motion produced a loud jarring of the earthen ware. The Pedlar awaked in confternation, and fnatching his whip, be-gan to lafh the Afs with mercilefs fury. The poor beaft fled from his ftripes, and was heard of no more; the panniers were thrown off; and the Burflem ware was

entirely

entirely demolifhed. Thus did inhumanity, lazinefs and paffion meet with deferved punifhment. Had the Pedlar remembered the craving hunger of the Afs, when he gratified his own; or had he purfued with diligence his journey after finifhing his repaft, no part of thefe misfortunes would have befallen him. And his lofs might have been inconfiderable, if unjuft feverity and rafh refentment had not compleated his ruin.

The BEES.

A DUTCH merchant who was fettled at Batavia procured a hive of young bees from Poland, that he might multiply the breed of this induftrious infect, and regale himfelf with honey prepared under his own infpection. The bees were ftationed in a delightful garden, of large extent, and furnifhed with the richeft profufion of fragrant herbs and flowers. Plenty foon corrupted their difpofition to labour; and the ftock of honey which they collected,

during

during the firſt months of their ſettlement,
was of little value.   The expected winter
did not enſue: and as they continued to
enjoy abundance in this happy climate,
they became improvident of futurity, and
were no longer at the pains to ſtore their
cells with that food, which bountiful nature at all ſeaſons provided for them.   Thus
unfavourable was exceſſive abundance to
the admired virtues of the Bee.   And no
leſs injurious to many a well-formed youth
is that affluence, which hath been heaped
together by parental toil, to gratify parental ambition; but which ſerves either
to nouriſh ſloth, by ſuperſeding the neceſ-
ſity of application; or to promote diſſipation, riot, and profligacy, by giving a
falſe direction to activity.

An   E P I T A P H.

T O

T H E   M E M O R Y

O F

S Y L V I A ;

A   C H E A R F U L   C O M P A N I O N ;

F A I T H F U L   F R I E N D ;

AND

AND

TRUE PHILOSOPHER;

IF SUBMISSION TO GOD,

BENEVOLENCE TO MAN,

AND

STRICT CONFORMITY TO NATURE,

WITH UNAFFECTED INDIFFERENCE

TO

PROFIT, POWER, OR FAME,

BE GENUINE PHILOSOPHY.

SHE

MINGLED IN ALL COMPANIES,

YET PRESERVED

HER NATIVE SIMPLICITY OF MANNERS;

AND WAS CARESSED BY THE PROFLIGATE,

WHILST SHE REPROVED THEIR

VICES

BY HER GOOD EXAMPLE.

HER RELIGION

WAS UNTAINTED WITH BIGOTRY,

ALTHOUGH SHE DOUBTED OF NO

ARTICLE OF FAITH:

AND

SHE STEADILY MAINTAINED

PASSIVE OBEDIENCE AND NON RESISTANCE,

WITHOUT BECOMING

A PARTIZAN IN POLITICS.

SPOTLESS AS A SAINT

SHE LIVED;

AND DIED A

MARTYR.

THIS

THIS MONUMENT
BLAZONS NO FEIGNED VIRTUES OF THE
DEAD,
TO FLATTER THE VANITY OF THE
LIVING;
FOR IT IS ERECTED, NOT TO A
WOMAN
BUT
A SPANIEL. *(z)*

ART thou offended, gentle reader, at this tribute to the memory of a faithful dog? Vifit the gardens at Stowe; and perufe the lines infcribed by Cobham to Signior Fido, his Italian greyhound! Or if Claffic Authority influence thy tafte, turn to the page of Plutarch, and read the following narration! " When the Atheni-
" ans, during the war in which they were
" engaged againft the Perfians, were con-
" ftrained to abandon their city, and retire
" to the ifland of Salamis, Xanthippus,
" the father of Pericles, embarked with
" the reft of his countrymen. His faith-
" ful dog, having been left behind, fwam
" after the fhip till he reached the fhore;
" where

(z) See an account of this Spaniel, part II. page 154.

" where the poor creature was no fooner
" landed than he threw himfelf down, ex-
" haufted with fatigue, and expired at his
" mafter's feet. Xanthippus buried him
" on the fpot; and as a grateful memorial
" of his fidelity, erected a monument over
" his grave, which remains to this day, and
" is known by the name of *Cynoffema*, or
" the dog's fepulchre."

IMMODERATE STUDY.

SOPHRON had paffed the day in very intenfe application to his favourite ftudy. The fhades of the evening infenfibly ftole upon him. He called for his lamp, and fupplied it with an extraordinary quantity of oil, that it might burn till midnight. The flame was languid and glimmering.—He added more oil—It yielded a ftill fainter light. Again he replenifhed the lamp—The flame became dimmer—He clofed his book; and was foon left in total darknefs.

AH !

AH! ftudious youth, ufe not with fuch profufion the facred oil of learning! Thus lavifhly applied it will extinguifh, not brighten the intellectual lamp that burns within thee.

THE CANARY BIRD AND RED LINNET.

ONE fine evening, in the month of May, a canary bird was carried into the garden at Hart Hill. The cage was fufpended by the branch of a cherry tree, the bloffoms and leaves of which overfpread the top of it, furnifhing at once a delightful fhade and luxurious repaft. I fat down near it on a bank of turf, and was highly pleafed to obferve how much the little creature feemed to enjoy his new fituation. After fluttering his wings, hopping about, and pecking the bloffoms which prefented themfelves through the wires of the cage, he at length fixed himfelf upon his perch, and began the moft melodious fong I ever heard. His notes were fo tuneful, diftinct, and various, that he foon filenced the

mufic

mufic of a neighbouring fhrubbery; and drew feveral birds into the cherry-tree. The fong of the canary was now interrupted by a loud chirping, which proceeded, as I could clearly difcern through the leaves of the tree, from a red linnet perched on a twig, almoft clofe to the cage. When the linnet ceafed, the canary bird feemed to reply by chirping in a fimilar manner, but with more fweetnefs and compofure. Imagination foon made me acquainted with this new language, and I fuppofed the following dialogue to have been carried on between them.

LINNET. Silly Bird! what caufe haft thou to raife fuch chearful and exulting notes? Compare with ours thy wretched fituation. And when thou vieweft the bleffings that we poffefs, fhew at leaft fome fhare of wifdom and fenfibility, by lamenting thy incapacity of attaining them. To rejoice in calamity is, furely, the height of folly.

CANARY BIRD. Your reproofs are cruel

T   and

and unjuſt. It is over the comforts, and not the evils of my ſituation, that I rejoice. When I ſee you roving at large, I feel the loſs of liberty; and as I hop from one ſide of my priſon to another, I often expand my wings, conſcious of powers which I am reſtrained from exerciſing. Nor am I indifferent to thoſe ſocial pleaſures, of which though ſometimes a witneſs, I am ſeldom a partaker. But why ſhould I repine that, in theſe reſpects, you are more happy than my ſelf! As reaſonably might you complain that partial Heaven has conferred advantages on me, which are denied to you. For in that ſeaſon when you are expoſed to hardſhip, famine, and danger, I am fed with a liberal hand; ſheltered from the winter's cold; and protected from the fowler, and every animal of prey. Allow me then, without reproach, to expreſs my thankfulneſs to God in ſongs of praiſe; to bear my lot with chearful reſignation; and even to rejoice in that good, which, though withholden from me, is beſtowed upon others of the feathered race.

IMPRESSED

IMPRESSED with thefe ideas, I arofe
from my feat, and retired to my chamber,
pondering the leffon of benevolence, gratitude, and contentment which I had heard.
My window commanded the view of a rich
and extenfive plain, bounded by lofty
mountains. The fun particularly illumined
a craggy cliff, the fummit and fides of
which were covered with pine trees. Fancy
was on the wing, and inftantly tranfported
me to the ftriking fcene. I conceived it
to be the refidence of Theophilus; and as
I entered the favourite grove of the pious
philofopher, his evening meditations thus
faluted my intellectual ear.—" Teach me
" to love Thee, and thy divine adminiftra-
" tion! to regard the univerfe itfelf as my
" true and genuine country, not that little
" cafual fpot where I firft drew vital air.
" Teach me to regard myfelf but as a part
" of this great whole; a part which for its
" welfare I am as patiently to refign, as I
" refign a fingle limb for the welfare of my
" whole body. Let my life be a continued
" fcene of acquiefcence and of gratitude;
" of gratitude for what I enjoy; of acqui-

T 2   " efcence

" efcence in what I fuffer; as both can
" only be referable to that concatenated
" order of events, which cannot but be
" beft, as being by thee approved and
" chofen.

" INASMUCH as futurity is hidden from
" my fight, I can have no other rule of
" choice, by which to govern my conduct,
" than what feems confonant to the welfare
" of my own particular nature. If it ap-
" pear not contrary to duty and moral
" office (and how fhould I judge but from
" what appears?) thou canft not but for-
" give me if I prefer health to ficknefs;
" the fafety of life and limb to maiming or
" to death. But did I know that thefe
" incidents, or any were appointed me, in
" that order of uncontroulable events, by
" which thou preferveft and adorneft the
" whole; it then becomes my duty to meet
" them with magnanimity; to co-operate
" with chearfulnefs in what thou ordaineft;
" that fo I may know no other will than
" thine alone, and that the harmony of
" my particular mind with thy univerfal
                                    " may

" may be fteady and uninterrupted through
" the period of my exiftence.

" YET fince to attain this height, this
" tranfcendant height, is but barely pof-
" fible, if poffible, to the moft perfect
" humanity ; regard what within me is
" congenial to Thee ; raife me above my-
" felf and warm me into enthufiafm. But
" let my enthufiafm be fuch as befits a
" citizen of thy polity ; liberal, gentle,
" rational, and humane—not fuch as to
" debafe me into a poor and wretched flave,
" as if thou wert my tyrant, not my father ;
" much lefs fuch as to transform me into a
" favage beaft of prey, fullen, gloomy,
" dark, and fierce ; prone to perfecute, to
" ravage, and deftroy, as if the luft of
" maffacre could be grateful to thy good-
" nefs. Permit me rather madly to avow
" villainy in thy defiance, than impioufly
" to affert it under colour of thy fervice.
" Turn my mind's eye from every idea of
" this character ; from the fervile, abject,
" horrid, and ghaftly, to the generous,
" lovely, fair, and godlike.

HERE

" Here let me dwell; — be here my
" ftudy and delight. So fhall I be enabled
" in the filent mirrour of contemplation to
" behold thofe forms which are hidden to
" human eyes — that animating wifdom
" which pervades and rules the whole ;
" that law irrefiftible, immutable, fupreme,
" which leads the willing, and compels
" the averfe, to co-operate in their ftation
" to the general welfare ; that magic divine
" which, by an efficacy paft comprehenfion,
" can transform every appearance, the moft
" hideous, into beauty, and exhibit all
" things fair and good to Thee, Effence
" Increate, *who art of purer eyes than ever*
" *to behold iniquity*.

" Be thefe my morning, thefe my evening
" meditations—with thefe may my mind
" be unchangeably tinged — that loving
" thee with a love moft difinterefted and
" fincere; enamoured of thy polity, and
" thy divine adminiftration ; welcoming
" every event with chearfulnefs and mag-
" nanimity as being beft upon the whole,
" becaufe ordained of Thee; propofing
" nothing

" nothing to myfelf but with a referve that
" Thou permitteft; acquiefcing in every
" obftruction as ultimately referable to thy
" providence — in a word, that working
" this conduct, by due exercife, into per-
" fect habit; I may never murmur, never
" repine; never mifs what I would obtain,
" nor fall into that which I would avoid;
" but be happy with that tranfcendent
" happinefs of which no one can deprive
" me; and bleft with that divine liberty
" which no tyrant can annoy." (a)

An EXPERIMENT.

LOOK attentively at this glafs, and
mark the variety of images which it
exhibits? You will fee in it the haughty
and infolent courtier, awed into gentlenefs
by the prefence of the tyrant, whom he
ferves: And the tyrant difturbed by fufpicion, fear, and anxiety, whilft he receives

T 4 with

(a) The paragraphs marked by inverted commas, have
been copied, with a few variations, from Mr. Harris's Dialogue
concerning Happinefs.

with ſmiles the incenſe of flattery, and
glories in his ſplendour and power: The
envious man tortured at the heart, yet ex-
preſſing outward ſigns of pleaſure, when
the merits of his rival are extolled: The
well educated youth, who has been ſeduced
by vicious companions, inwardly appalled
during the hours of riot and jollity: The
idle lounger, ſeemingly at eaſe, but really
fretful, diſcontented, and unhappy.

— You are jocular, ſaid Alexis. I ſee
nothing but a glaſs tumbler, containing
about two parts of water and one of oil,
ſuſpended by a cord, and ſwung backwards
and forwards by your hand. The oil appears perfectly ſmooth and undiſturbed,
whilſt the water below is in violent agitation.

And do you not perceive, anſwered
Euphronius, a ſtriking analogy between
this internal ſtorm but ſuperficial calm,
and the ſeveral characters which I have
enumerated?—I will diverſify the alluſion,
and vary the experiment by pouring out
                                        the

the oil, and fupplying its place with water.
The fluid, you obferve, now remains tran
quil throughout, although the fame motion
is given to the veffel as before. *(b)* Thus
compofure of mind may be preferved
amidſt the agitations and tumults of life,
if we cherifh no paffions, that, like oil and
water, are difcordant to each other.—Alexis acknowledged the propriety of thefe
moral analogies ; but expreffed his furprize
and perplexity at the appearances from
which they were deduced. He was defired
to confider them attentively, and to exercife his genius in the folution of them.

The ROVING FISHES.

" IF folid happinefs we prize,
" Within our breaſt this jewel lies,
    " And they are fools who roam. ————

" Of reſt was Noah's dove bereft,
" When, with impatient wing, fhe left
    " That fafe retreat, the Ark :
" Giving her vain excurfion o'er,

                                " The

(b) See **Dr.** Franklin's Experiments and Obfervations on
Electricity.

" The difappointed bird once more
" Explor'd the facred bark."*(c)*

Sophronia, whofe maternal tendernefs
was directed by a folid judgment and
well cultivated underftanding, had been
repeating thefe lines to her fon, and urging
the difficulties, temptations, and dangers
which await the inexperienced youth, when
he too forwardly launches into the bufy
world. They were enjoying an evening's
walk ; and the path which they purfued terminated in a beautiful pond, fupplied with water by a murmuring rill,
that for a while feemed to lofe its current, but paffing onwards flowed, through
a concealed grate, into a neighbouring
brook. Having reached the margin of
the pond, they ftopped to gaze at the
fportive fifhes, gliding in all directions,
with graceful eafe, through the yielding
element. But a large tench was obferved
to remain in one unvaried pofition, as if
ftupified with pain, or overwhelmed with
forrow. Were fifhes capable of reflection,
I fhould

(c) Cotton's Fire-Side.

I fhould prefume, faid Sophronia, that the tench, we are looking at, is mourning the folly and calamities of her offspring. Laſt week, a fudden and unufual fwell of the brook raifed the water of this pond above its level; and three young tench eagerly took the opportunity of efcaping over the grate, and quitted with joy the confinement, to which they had fubmitted for fome time with impatience and difcontent. They fwam down the ſtream, exulting in their liberty; and were juſt entering a fpacious mill pool, which promifed every gratification to their boundlefs wifhes, when a ravenous pike feized upon the foremoſt, and terrified the others with the apprehenfion of dangers before unknown. The fhallows of the pool were now fought, for fecurity; but the flood having damaged the dike, the water rapidly difcharged itfelf. One of the remaining tench was left in a hollow, to die a painful and lingering death; the other, impelled by hunger, fwallowed a bait, and became the prey of a fifherman. Thus perifhed thefe unfortunate rovers; affording us a leffon of inftruction,

ftruction, concluded Sophronia, which it
cannot be neceffary either to explain or to
apply.

The HISTORIAN and the PAINTER.

WHAT unpleafing face is this, faid
an Hiftorian to a Painter, as he
was viewing the exhibition of his pictures?
It is the portrait, anfwered the artift, of a
man whom I fecretly defpife, and I have
purpofely rendered it harfh and difagreeable.—What a liberal and noble countenance, continued the learned fpectator,
does the picture before me difplay? So
looks the original, replied the Painter;
and I have the honour to call him my
friend and patron.—May I not prefume,
then, that the Venus, on the right hand,
is the likenefs of your miftrefs? I confefs
it, faid the artift with a blufh. But if
paffion and prejudice fometimes guide my
pencil, how much more frequently do they
direct your pen? I delineate chiefly for
the eye; you for the underftanding and
the

the heart. To deceive, therefore, may be *venial* in the Painter, but is *criminal* in the Hiftorian. The art of falfe colouring, however, is not peculiar either to you or to me. It is practifed by all mankind, both in their judgments of themfelves and of others. Self-love ftrongly incites to draw a flattering picture; political and religious prejudices, though lefs forcible, are not lefs certain in their influence; and envy, rivalfhip, and hatred offer to our pencil only dark and difgufting taints.

"All is infected that th' infected fpy,
"As all looks yellow to the jaundiced eye."

THE RATTLE SNAKE.

AN European youth, fauntering through a wood in Virginia, heedlefs where he trod, fuddenly heard a harfh rattling noife, which filenced the warbling of the nightingales, and feemed to ftrike terror into every living object around him. He looked forward, and beheld, acrofs the path which he purfued, a large fnake, with the

the head erect, the body coiled, and the tail, from which the found proceeded, in continual agitation. Alarmed with the danger that awaited him, he haftenend back to Williamfburgh; and was eager both to recount his adventure, and to give utterance to the reflections which it had fuggefted. How wife, faid he, are the provifions of the Author of Nature, to guard his favourite man from whatever may prove noxious or deftructive to him? The lion roars when he iffues from his den; the wolf howls in his nocturnal ex-curfions; and the dreadful ferpent, from which I efcaped this morning, fhakes his rattle, as he crawls along, to warn us of the danger that approaches.

Ceafe, young man, replied a venerable fage, to accufe Providence of partiality; nor abufe the wifdom of God, by applaufes which are founded only on pride and igno-rance. The animals, you have mentioned, inhabit many a defart where no human footftep can be traced: How then fhould their inftincts or exertions have any refer-
ence

ence to the fecurity of man! The lions
roar, and the wolves howl to roufe the
beafts from their fecret hiding places: For
without fuch difcovery of their prey, of
what avail would be their ftrength or
fwiftnefs.

The fnake, you faw, produces no found
with its tail, in the ordinary motions of his
body; and had not a childifh fear prevented you might have been a witnefs to the
ufe which he makes of his rattle. That
reptile feeds chiefly on fquirrels and birds,
which he cannot catch without fome artifice
to bring them within his reach. He therefore creeps near the tree, on whofe branches
he perceives them; and fuddenly fhaking
his rattle, fo affrights the poor creatures on
which he fixes his piercing eyes, that they
have no power to efcape. And they leap
from bough to bough till, overcome with
terror and fatigue, they fall to the ground,
and are devoured by their ravenous enemy. (d)

An

(d) See Mead on Poifons.

An EXPERIMENT.

TWO young beech trees, planted at the fame time, in the fame foil, at a fmall diftance from each other, and equally healthy, were pitched upon as the fubjects of the following experiment. They were accurately meafured ; and as foon as the buds began to fwell in the fpring, the whole trunk of one of them was cleanfed of its mofs and dirt, by means of a brufh and foft water. Afterwards it was wafhed with a wet flannel, twice or thrice every week, till about the middle of fummer. In autumn, when the annual growth was fuppofed to be compleated, the beeches were again meafured ; and the increafe of the tree which had beed wafhed was found to exceed that of the other nearly in the proportion of two to one. (e)

HAD you feen the commencement of
this

(e) See Dr. Hales's Statical Effays; Mr. Evelyn's Silva ; and the Philofophical Tranfactions, Vol. 67.

this experiment, Alexis, you would probably have fmiled at the *nicety* of the
gardener, and thought his labour mifap-
plied. But the conclufion of it will give
you different ideas; and perhaps convince
you, by the obvious analogy, that cleanli-
nefs and frequent wafhing promote the
health, vigour, and growth of the body.
It may fatisfy you alfo, that various minute
attentions, in the conduct of your education, which at prefent may feem to be
fuperfluous and irkfome, are of real importance, by removing thofe caufes which
would retard your progrefs towards manly
ftrength and mental excellence. For every
habit of aukwardnefs impairs fome ufeful
power of action; and as the mofs preys on
the nutritious juices of the beech, fo falfe
opinions and principles defpoil the mind
of a correfpondent portion of knowledge,
truth, and virtue.

TRUE

TRUE ELEVATION OF MIND DISPLAYED IN
CONDESCENSION AND HUMANITY.

SIR Philip Sydney was one of the
brighteſt ornaments of Queen Eliza-
beth's court. In early youth he difcovered
the ſtrongeſt marks of genius and under-
ſtanding. Sir Fulk Greville, Lord Brook,
who was his intimate friend, and who has
written an account of his life, ſays,
"Though I lived with him, and knew him
"from a child, yet I never knew him other
"than a man; with ſuch ſteadineſs of
"mind, lovely and familiar gravity, as car-
"ried grace and reverence above greater
"years. His talk was ever of knowledge,
"and his very play, tended to enrich his
"mind."

HE was an active ſupporter of the cauſe
of liberty in the Low Countries, where
he had a command, under his uncle the
Earl of Leiceſter, general of the Engliſh
forces employed againſt the tyrant Philip
the II. of Spain. In the battle near Zutphen
he

he difplayed the moft undaunted and en-
terprifing courage. He had two horfes
killed under him, and whilft mounting a
third was wounded by a mufket-fhot out
of the trenches, which broke the bone of
his thigh. He returned about a mile and
a half on horfeback to the camp; and being faint with the lofs of blood, and probably parched with thirft through the
heat of the weather, he called for drink.
It was prefently brought to him: but as
he was putting the veffel to his mouth,
a poor wounded foldier, who happened
to be carried by him at that inftant, looked
up to it with wifhful eyes. The gallant and
generous Sydney took the bottle from his
mouth, juft when he was going to drink,
and delivered it to the foldier, faying,
" *thy neceffity is yet greater than mine.*"
Sir Philip was conveyed to Arnheim, and
attended by the principal furgeons of the
camp. During fixteen days great hopes
were entertained of his recovery; but the
ball not being extracted, and a mortification enfuing, he prepared himfelf for
death with the utmoft piety and fortitude;

and

and expired on the 17th of October, 1586, in the thirty second year of his age. He is said to have taken leave of his brother in these affecting terms: " Love my me-" mory; cherish my friends; their fide-" lity to me may assure you that they are " honest. But above all, govern your will " and affections, by the will and word of " your Creator; in me beholding the end " of this world, with all her vanities." *(f)*

SPECULATION AND PRACTICE.

" A CERTAIN Astronomer was con-" templating the moon through " his telescope, and tracing the extent of " her seas, the height of her mountains, " and the number of habitable territories " which she contains. Let him spy what " he pleases, said a clown to his compa-" nion; he is not nearer to the moon " than we are."*(g)*

SHALL the same observation be made of you, Alexis? Do you surpass others in learning,

(f) See the British Biography, vol. VI. Article Sydney.
(g) Harris on Happiness.

learning, and yet in goodnefs remain upon a level with the uninftructed vulgar? Have you fo long gazed at the temple of virtue, without advancing one ftep towards it? Are you fmitten with moral beauty, yet regardlefs of its attainment? Are you a philofopher in theory, but a novice in practice? The partiality of a father inclines me to hope, that the reverfe is true. I flatter myfelf that by having learned to think, you will be qualified to act; and that the rectitude of your conduct will be adequate to your improvements in knowledge. May that wifdom, which is juftified in her works, be your guide through life! And may you enjoy all the felicity which flows from a cultivated underftanding, well regulated affections, extenfive benevolence, and amiable manners! In thefe confift that fovereign good, which ancient fages fo much extol; which reafon recommends, religion authorifes, and God approves.

THE END.

For EU product safety concerns, contact us at Calle de José Abascal, 56–1°, 28003 Madrid, Spain or eugpsr@cambridge.org.

www.ingramcontent.com/pod-product-compliance
Ingram Content Group UK Ltd.
Pitfield, Milton Keynes, MK11 3LW, UK
UKHW010349140625
459647UK00010B/940